PAINKILLER – BRAINKILLER

Written by James M Powers II

Completed 12/14/2023

DISCLAIMER

This book is a memoir based on true events. It reflects my

present recollections of experiences over time. Some names and

characters have been changed. Some events have been

compressed and some dialogue has been recreated. I have tried

to recreate events, locales and conversations from my memories

of them. In order to maintain their anonymity in some instances

I have changed the names of Individuals and places. I may have

changed some identifying characteristics and details , such as

physical properties, occupation, and place of resident. This

memoir is a truthful and honest recollection of actual events that

happened in my life. Some conversations have been recreated

and/or supplemented. The names and details of certain

individuals have been changed to protect their privacy. I have made every attempt to provide information that is accurate and complete. This book is not intended as a substitute for professional medical advice. The book is not meant to be used nor should it be used to diagnose and/or treat any medical condition or psychological condition. Readers are advised to consult their own medical advisors and doctors whose responsibility is to determine the condition of and the best treatment for the reader.

DEDICATION

I dedicate this book to my two most devoted Cancer zodiac-signed fans: my mother, Margaret Ann, who has spent more of her time in prayer for me than all the Popes have in the last century. She's nothing short of an angel! And my wife Melanie, whose love and unwavering support kept me going through this journey. She was the one who pushed me to write my story, hoping it could help others facing similar struggles. Without them, these pages would have never come together. I'd also like to thank my late father, who stood by me through some tough times. He may have had a hard exterior, but his heart was soft; most fathers would have simply written off their son as a mistake, but he didn't do that with me. He stood by me and gave me the time to work it out. I don't think I could've been as strong as he was. Most of the time, we had so much fun together. Those were some of my favorite days! Even when things were tough, he had my back. I love and miss you Podge, save me a spot in heaven. Last, Tallula Lucille Powers, our beautiful daughter. She is our ten-pound bundle of joy from up above. They sent us a Brussels Griffon straight from heaven.

INTRODUCTION

The pages that are forthcoming are my personal 28-year-roller coaster ride straight into the depths of hell and into the belly of the beast himself! Into the everlasting darkness of pain pill addiction. This book is not like most stories you have read. I not only survived but kicked my pain pill addiction in the ass. The devil's ass at that! Just a quick disclaimer, do not be scared away by religious references. That is not what this book is about. Yes, I am a Christian. Christianity played a huge role in saving my life. That's my story and I would never expect my exact path to be yours. Your religious affiliation or even lack of religious belief is not important to me. I am not here to cram my religious beliefs down your throat, convert you, or place judgment on you. I am here to tell my story so others struggling with addiction know they have a fighting chance at a brand new, beautiful life.

Now that we have that uncomfortable subject out of the way, let me be realistic and clarify a few things. Overnight miracles do not exist in overcoming this demon. This isn't an overnight hallelujah miracle performed by an enigmatic tent revival preacher that claims to be touched by the hand of God. No magical force came over me and healed me" If only it was that easy! This is a continuous 28 year battle I have fought daily since my auto accident in 1995! The first three quarters of this book contain everything I did while in the grip of my addiction, which I'm sure the Devil enjoyed.

It provides you with some fantastic and perplexing reading as well! It's one crazy ass true story, trust me! The entire time I sat wondering which day I would die! If Vegas would have laid odds on me surviving and writing a book explaining how I have won this 28 year battle. The odds against me would be astronomical. People always say things like "it is 1 million to one", that's merely a cliche. My odds would have been something like 5 million to one. As a gambler and poker player, I understand numbers and odds well. At 5 million to one, I still wouldn't have bet on myself. Now give me 10 million to one. Maybe I might bet a dollar or two. All bullshit aside, I wouldn't wish this addiction on my worst enemy. It is a real life nightmare you live day after day after day! What I can do, though, is tell you my story and give you one hell of a blueprint on how to beat this monster. I can't crawl into the cage with you when you battle this beast, though. You yourself have to do that. If you want it bad enough, you too can win this battle! I did and there isn't anything special about me or my addiction. Another opiate addict, living in the cruel depths of hell! Ok, so let's start this story. "Ladies and gentlemen this is your captain speaking, please buckle your seatbelts, put your tray tables and seatbacks in their upright position and get ready for a turbulent 15 year ride on Narcotic express airlines!

"How well I have learned that there is no fence to sit on between heaven and hell. There is a deep, wide gulf, a chasm, and in that chasm is no place for any man"

Johnny Cash

Chapter 1

Who The Hell Are You?!

Please allow me to introduce myself: I'm a man of wealth and taste. Oh, I'm sorry, that's Mick Jagger. I'm no rockstar, that's for sure. Instead, it is just another statistic adding to the number of folks addicted to pain pills. My name is James Marion Powers II, born on June 9th, 1963 in Lexington KY. My parents adopted me at six weeks old. To this day, I do not know of my birth parents. My mother was fourteen and my father was seventeen years old. Out of fear of what her family would think, my mother had to hide her pregnancy from the world for nine months. I've been told that my birth mother was from a prominent family and had no other choice than to leave town to have me in order to protect herself and her loved ones from judgment and disgrace. When I was six weeks old, Kenneth Powers and Margaret Ann Powers, who became my mother and father, adopted me. The two of them have been an incredible blessing in my life. God sent me angels when they chose me as their son. Especially my mom; she has been the reason I'm still alive today.

My father was a good man, strong-willed but kind. I tragically lost him in February 2022. More than anything, I wish that I could speak to him just one last time! My addiction caused me to waste too much precious time, time that I can never regain! Over several years, I was estranged because of my substance abuse; however, in the last five years before his passing, we became closer than ever. I love you always, Podge. Hold a spot up there for me.

My parents got divorced in 1974 and they awarded my father sole custody of me. Why, you might ask? Well, he had threatened to kill my mother if she didn't agree to this arrangement. I have since forgiven him for that horrendous action. He gave me a good life as a child, which is all I can ask for. After the divorce, he took me to Florida so he could manage a horse farm there. In retrospect, I strongly believe he did this mainly to piss off my mom. We stayed for three years before returning to Kentucky, where I went to high school and then on to Eastern Kentucky University on a football scholarship. Having six hundred acres of land to play on during those three years was so much fun.

I want to clarify that my story is not one of some tragic childhood or unhappiness that made me turn to drugs as a way of coping. I had a beautiful childhood. One could even say it was idyllic. As a kid, I had a normal level of curiosity about exploring recreational substances, but nothing greater than usual. It wasn't until I was thirty-two years old that I became truly addicted after being in a car accident. This book's purpose is to give hope to those going through similar struggles with addiction; if only one person finds this book beneficial, it has served its purpose.

I'm determined to get this message out; there is still hope! Pain pill, opiate addiction can make you feel you've lost all hope when you're down in the deep, dark cavernous hole it pulls you into. You may feel like life is pointless and that you'll never escape your addiction. Hope is the everlasting key. Always have hope because when you've lost hope, the game is over! You feel as if you're never going to get better and life is very black. Life feels like a void. I know I have been in that dark, nasty hell hole! I have been in the bottom of that pit crying and screaming for mercy. Exactly where you could be today! I have felt that hopelessness, but you can beat this shit. I did!

NOW, stop reading and shut your eyes to say this quick prayer:

Dear God (Higher Power), please help me/my friend to overcome this addiction. Grant me the courage I need to vanquish this vice and make it through.

Be my ray of hope and my guide through this darkness,

Amen.

Having been through it myself, I'm sure you can conquer the addiction. The narrative in this book reflects your own journey. I believe that you will make it out alive. My ultimate wish is that you, like me, will crush this demon called pain pill addiction and rip it apart limb by limb.

"The difference between here and there is hardly any distance at all."

Mark Twain

Chapter 2

The Wreck

I told Ryan I'd be at the golf course in thirty minutes and went downtown to the Hyatt. It was such a glorious day; I couldn't help but appreciate it. Just before I reached a red stoplight, I hung up the phone with Ryan. That's when I reached down and changed the station on the radio. Suddenly, everything went dark, and I awoke with a medic waving smelling salts under my nose.

"Where am I??? What happened???" I thought as my eyes took in the ambulance's interior. The paramedic informed me I had been in a car accident. I had stopped at a red light when a woman crashed into the back of my car at a high speed. Miraculously, he said, I was lucky to be alive. I recalled leaving to go golfing just before the incident, and my mind raced with questions about my injuries. As best as I could from my position in the ambulance, I checked myself over and was relieved to find that: A. I didn't see any stabilizing cast of any kind. B. I had all my limbs that could have had a cast, and C. Had ten fingers and ten toes, and everything seemed to go to the correct position and was working correctly. They still put me together, just as the good Lord made me!

"I'm so thirsty," I told the paramedic as he handed me a water bottle. "How do you feel?" he enquired. "Everything appears to be working properly," I replied. "That's fantastic news," he said. "We're going to take you to the hospital to have everything examined." Considering how well I felt, I didn't think I had to go. "Well, sir, it's ultimately your decision. But I'd highly advise you to get checked out by a doctor," the EMT suggested. "I suppose I'm alright," I said. The EMT responded, "Okay then, it's your call." To my surprise, my old Chevy Blazer was still driveable. I remember thinking what a tough ass truck and hearing the song in my head, "Like A Rock" by Bob Segar. Those commercials in those days repeatedly played!." LIKE A ROCK; I WAS STRONG AS I COULD BE, LIKE A ROCK, BUT NOTHING EVER GOT TO ME."

The only thing that prevented further injury was the spare tire strapped to the back of my car. "I recommend you go to the hospital," the paramedic said again. The police officer standing next to him nodded in agreement. "I think I'll just try to relax at home, and if I don't feel better, I'll go to the hospital," I replied. "Okay, it is your choice, sir, but stay awake for the next few hours. You probably have a concussion." "No big deal", I thought. I had suffered plenty during my football career; undoubtedly, one more wouldn't hurt me.

"Got it," I said, standing and walking down to the back end of the ambulance. The entire width of my truck had caved in like an accordion, about two feet deep. There did not appear to be anything wrong with it when I pulled it into the Hyatt parking garage only a few moments ago. I sat in stunned silence as a sharp pain traveled down my neck and shoulders, worse than any injury I'd gotten from football. Soon after, the police wrapped up their investigation, and everyone dispersed as if nothing had happened. My neck continued to throb in agony. Luckily, my chiropractor friend (whom I would sometimes golf with) had his office only two miles away and possessed an X-ray-MRI machine. After arriving at the office, Terry warmly welcomed me inside.

"Damn, brother, you're white as a ghost," Terry said as I explained the chain of events that had just happened to me in the last hour. "Come back, and we can run some x-rays and MRI of your neck area." I uttered a quick "Thank you" before sitting back down. "You should have gone to the hospital," Terry said concernedly. Terry reappeared at the front of the room after analyzing the MRI and X-ray results. His face showed the gravity of the situation. "You have taken a hefty blow to both your head and neck when that girl rear-ended you," he declared. "NO SHIT!" I thought, but what came out was awkward, "Yeah, I know." Terry then showed me the X-ray on the wall. It all still felt very alien to me. I remember him saying, "You have a severe injury."

Fortunately, Terry had a good acquaintance, a neurosurgeon named Mark. His practice was at the hospital near the country club. Terry called his neurosurgeon friend to see if he could see me straight away. The tone of Terry's voice made me uneasy. I'd known him for years and had never heard him sound so melancholy. A melancholy that unnerved me even more than the car accident itself! "Is it that bad?" I asked. "Yes, it is," Terry replied. "You need to get checked out ASAP." Terry phoned the doctor, and a few minutes later, a man was on the other end. I couldn't understand all the medical terminology as Terry explained what he had read in my X-ray and MRI scan. Terry's tone conveyed a sense of seriousness. I wasn't used to this side of him.

"Thanks, Mark. I'll get Jimbo on this right away," Terry said. Terry then gave an address and a stern warning: "Jimbo, don't mess around with this if you want to keep walking and playing golf." Terry's words hit me like a ton of bricks. The reality of my injury sank in, and it was obvious I should have gone to the hospital when I had the chance.

"One day, in retrospect, the years of struggle will strike you as the most beautiful."

Sigmund Freud

Chapter 3

Dr. Feel Good

The doctor's waiting room receptionist informed me they had an opening available in August. Terry, my chiropractor buddy, had warned me that if I bumped my head again, it would paralyze me from the waist down, and that's all I could think of. "I need to see you guys as soon as possible," I said. The receptionist nodded before calling Terry, who had referred me, to ensure it was okay. As the receptionist spoke on the phone, her expression changed, and she became pale. The nurse's pallor wasn't a good sign.

"Please stay put, Mr. Powers," the receptionist said before leaving the room. After what felt like an eternity, she returned and pointed me to a chair; the doctor would be with me soon. A nurse opened the doctor's exam room door and gestured for me to enter before I could inquire about why they rescheduled my appointment to an earlier date. As soon as I stepped inside, I saw they adorned every wall with pictures of what lies beneath our skin and smiles: the inner workings of our bodies. The nurse silently left as soon as she closed the door.

As I immersed myself in all the detailed knowledge about the human body, someone walked into the room and greeted me as "Mr. Powers." I could not help but think, "Is this another doctor who will point out how lucky I am?" What's so fortunate in being involved in a car accident that was not my fault? The doctor explained my injuries in greater detail while using some pointing device like those professors use when showing something on a chalkboard. Wanting him to continue, I replied with a small smile, "Yes sir, I understand."

As the doctor pointed out different parts of the skeletal diagram, I couldn't help but feel a bit confused. After about ten minutes, the doctor asked if I understood, making me roll my eyes. It was ridiculous that even though he explained how they would fix my neck, I could only think about the TV show I watched as a kid called

The Six-Million Dollar Man. Like Lee Majors in the show, the doctor could make me better, stronger, faster.

A slight smirk appeared as I replied, "Yes, sir. I understand." "Perfect," the doctor said, "We'll schedule the surgery for next Friday at 3 pm." "Excellent," I responded. The doctor began prescribing Percocet to help me manage the pain. Unfortunately, he didn't give me the warning I needed about how addictive and dangerous this drug could be. Instead, he said, "The nurse will bring your prescription in a few minutes. If you need anything before then, call our office anytime." As I stood up, an electric bolt shot down my spine, jolting me from head to toe. "Damn," I thought aloud, "I need to get those Percocet now and find some relief."

I started toward the country club, where I'd spent many hours in the past. Only then did it finally sink in how much my life had changed, and it overcame me with fear, something foreign to me. Playing golf seemed distant and uncertain. Questions filled my head as I pulled out of the parking lot. Would I ever be able to hit a golf ball again? An urgent sense of sadness washed over me until I reminded myself, at least you're not paralyzed, and drove the short two miles to pick up my prescription at the pharmacy.

My mind wandered as I entered the pharmacy, which had the atmosphere of an old apothecary from the beginning of the 19th century. After handing my prescription to the young man at the front desk, he told me it would be about five minutes before it was ready. I glanced at my watch and felt a wave of sadness overcome me as I thought about how much time I usually spent playing golf. A few minutes later, an older gentleman, who made Mr Whipple look like a serial killer, approached me with my filled prescription. When I took out a twenty-dollar bill to pay him, he asked if I had ever taken Percocet. When I said no, the pharmacist warned me they might make me dizzy and not to drive while taking them. Chills ran down my spine as I walked out of the pharmacy and back to my car. Looking back, I understand why. I wonder what would have happened if the pharmacist had given me even a small lecture on what this medication could do to me. Would I have still gone down this treacherous path?

It's not his fault, that was back in 1996. This was before the evil monster of opioid addiction had been at the forefront of everyone's mind. In the same year, society also witnessed the emergence and release of the demon known as OxyContin.

Would a five-minute lecture have changed things for me then? Probably not. I remember how amazing it felt when that evil snake called opioids hit my bloodstream and traveled its way to the dopamine bullseye center. It was overwhelming, actually mind-blowing how good it made me feel. Until now, I never knew that such a feeling existed, let alone that I could experience and continue to handle it.

On my drive home, I stopped at a red light and read the label on my prescription bottle; it said to take one or two tablets every four to six hours as needed for pain. My neck suddenly started hurting—not enough to warrant taking drugs, but it still hurt. The doctor prescribed them, so surely they couldn't be wrong for me, right?

I grabbed a bottle from the shelf and quickly popped it open, thinking I should take two since I weighed 230 pounds. Thirty minutes later, a sensation of security settled in my mind with an intensity unlike anything I had ever experienced. Suddenly, I felt like a superhero. Nothing could stop me. When I stepped inside my house, even the kids and the dog that usually annoyed me seemed to be on my side. My wife asked how my doctor's appointment went— all I said was that they scheduled a minor surgery for my neck, but it was nothing to worry about. As I was lying down to rest, the song "Don't Worry, Be Happy" looped in my head until I eventually drifted off to sleep.

"Wisdom comes alone only through suffering."

Aeschylus

Chapter 4

Tee It High and Let It Fly

The next day was Country Club Day at Power's house. We

would play golf, my wife and kids would go to the pool, and then we would attempt to eat dinner all together. As I bent down to tie my shoes, I felt a sharp pain in my neck. I thought silently; I hope it's not too bad for me to play today. As I made the two-minute walk from my house to the golf course, I remembered the Percocet the doctor had prescribed me yesterday in case of any pain. Well, this pain qualified, so I took two pills and put the others into my golf bag before continuing on my way.

About a half hour to forty-five minutes later, I felt a familiar euphoria. While I waited for my friends to play golf, my mind was wandering as the mind-blowing effects of the poppy plant started dancing in my head. I thought to myself, what is in this small pill that made me feel so good? "Man, I love these things." ran through my brain. Looking back on it now, all it took were two little pills to ruin my life nearly. As I asked my golf buddies if they had ever taken Percocet, they replied, "Why, do you have some?". I passed them out like a roll of lifesavers and quickly discovered they were precisely like Lay's potato chips. No one could eat just one! After the third hole, you would have thought God had come down and granted all our prayers. No one had a problem or a care in the world.

Even after the sunset, we still played golf. We could barely see our golf carts, but we made it work. We didn't want the fun to end, so we kept going. Our Percocet-fueled adventure was beginning! They were now riding the Percocet Express with me! The following week flew by in a blur, and soon I was at the hospital, ready for my surgery.

"There is no harm in hoping for the best, as long as you're prepared for the worst."

Stephen King

Chapter 5

The Surgery

Early the following Friday morning, I prepared to leave for the

hospital. After downing a couple of Percocets and taking a shower, I

headed out to get checked in for my surgery. The nurse placed an IV

in my arm and injected me with 10 milligrams of valium, which

soon sent me into a state of euphoria. 'Have you had anything to eat or drink after midnight?" she asked me. I answered confidently, "No, ma'am."

A few minutes later, she returned with two syringes filled with drugs. "This will help you relax before surgery," she said as she slowly pushed the fluid into the IV in my hand. "What drugs are you giving me?" I asked, wanting to remember how they made me feel. She replied that one of them was an anti-nausea medication, and the other was Dilaudid for pain relief. OK, I responded, bracing myself as she carefully administered the first drug. The nurse found my bulging vein and inserted the second syringe into the IV. Instantly, a blanket of warmth enveloped my body and, soon after, my mind. It was one of the most satisfying feelings I had ever experienced, and I couldn't believe how great it was. The human body is something else; I never imagined the brain could feel that amazing. As she injected the Dilaudid into my IV, an indescribable and breathtaking sense of euphoria coursed through me.

My thoughts raced as I tried to make sense of the situation. Is this happening? The Percocet was OK, but it couldn't compare to the Dilaudid. Before I knew it, I was being wheeled into the operating room while my mind floated away. The surgeon appeared and asked how I felt, but all that came out was a weak, "Great, let's get this over with." The surgeon told me to count from ten as he prepared for the procedure. But counting down never worked for me; no matter how hard I tried, I always lost consciousness before reaching one. Suddenly, I awakened in the recovery room with a nurse by my side asking about my pain level. I answered truthfully and waited while she retrieved more medication. Soon enough, a rush of euphoria washed over me, a sensation unlike any other I had ever known. The nurse injected me with a potion, and it raced through my veins like an Indy 500 race car. I returned to that drugged state Pink Floyd sang about long ago. Comfortably numb. "Have you been to the restroom since your surgery?" the nurse questioned, and I silently thought: why did she ask that? When I said no, the nurse replied that if I didn't go soon, she'd have to put in a catheter. Whoa, why? My nurse explained how narcotics can make one numb and prevent urination. OK then, I'll try. After about 10 minutes, she returned to my room. "How's your pain now, Mr. Powers?" she requested without missing a beat, and I answered that the last shot had made little of a difference. I'd rate it at a 7. My nurse nodded and said she'd get more medication for me.

When I first tasted the magical elixir, I wondered how I'd feel with another shot. Not long after, I found out. It was a feeling beyond words—my mind raced with positive thoughts and feelings. When the nurse returned to check on me after about 20 minutes, she asked if I'd gone to the restroom. Again, I told her no, and she threatened me with a catheter once more. In that dreamy drug-induced state, everything seemed alright—the Dilaudid kept questions from entering my mind. Strange as it may sound, if you've experienced this drug before, you know exactly what I'm talking about! The nurse returned one last time in twenty minutes and repeated the same question.

When the nurse came back, I was going to tell her I had peed, though it wasn't true. I had no desire for a catheter; I had heard enough stories from men who'd had one. As expected, she reappeared around twenty minutes later with the same questions: "Are you in a lot of pain?" I answered affirmatively, feeling like my body slowly levitated from the bed. "Mr. Powers, I'm afraid to give you any more medication," she said cautiously, "In my 25 years of nursing, this is the most painkillers I've ever prescribed after an operation." My nurse said she had given me enough Dilaudid to put down a horse! I look back now and think that maybe I was close to overdosing - it's happened multiple times before where I would wake up coughing and gagging from vomit in my throat but feeling incredible, the best I've ever felt in my life. As I was trying to locate my heartbeat, I found that it was so slow that it seemed like it had stopped. I did not care. This was the best I have ever felt in my life.

I affirmed I was OK with seeing the sun come up tomorrow, and she left but then spun around. "Mr Powers," she asked, "Have you peed yet?" I lied and said yes, but she immediately saw through my bluff. The nurse came over and pushed down with her hand in my stomach somewhere and said, "No, you haven't." Then, the nurse came back a few minutes later with a catheter in hand and inserted it into me without me even realizing what was happening. Hell, you could have stuck a flathead screwdriver up my urethra, and I wouldn't have felt it.

Suddenly, the nurse said it was in place, and I had done my business. After about half an hour, my dad came to pick me up so I could start my recovery at his house.

" If you think you can or you can't, you're right."

Henry Ford

Chapter 6

I Want Them Now

☐　　The next few days passed by in a daze. My newfound buddy,

Mr. Percocet, accompanied me to my dad's house. It's possible that I ingested some during that afternoon. I actually could barely remember the ride home from the hospital, remembering that the nurse had told me she had given me more Dilaudid than anyone else after their surgery in her 25-year history as a nurse! The nurse said, "I have given you enough Dilaudid to knock a horse down." Therefore, I remember very little of that day.

The following morning, I awoke to an excruciating pain that made me scream when I attempted to get out of bed. "Are you okay?" my dad asked from downstairs. "Yeah, I'm fine," I answered, trying to recall the location of the genie bottle nearby. It felt like a bolt of lightning ran through my entire body, making it difficult to catch my breath. The jolt was not what I had expected from the operation; it was supposed to take away the electric shock and heal my neck. When the voltage stopped, I spotted the genie bottle on my nightstand. "Are you okay?" My dad questioned again from downstairs.

My brain told me I was ready as I put my hand on the bottle that held the genie. "I'm fine," I said before opening it and popping three Percocets. My brain had overridden my sensible side, telling me that more was better when something made me feel good! I disregarded the bottle's suggestion of taking one or two tablets every four to six hours for pain relief as my mind fixated on obtaining more narcotics. My emotions became a rollercoaster ride that I both loved and hated simultaneously. No matter what, I wanted that euphoric rush, and I would get it somehow. The baffling thing is every time I got that next bottle, my brain would always tell me, "Okay, now you can use this bottle to wean yourself off these things! This will be my last bottle". My brain rationalized this in my mind for 15 years. Of course, when I was experiencing withdrawal symptoms like sweating and diarrhea, my brain explained that the only way to take away the discomfort was to take even more. The problem is that your brain and body don't say the same thing when you're starting to withdraw. You sweat and feel you are defecating through a chicken wire fence! Your brain tells you, "Listen, do whatever you need to do not to feel this way." Unfortunately, the only way to relieve the pain is to swallow more of the devil's seed!

Did I go off on a tangent? My apologies. Where were we? The surgery! I tried my best to block it from my memory for reasons you are about to read. The surgery was a terrifying prospect. I had heard horrifying tales of botched surgeries, and the idea of experiencing one filled me with fear. I did my best to prepare myself. I'd done my research, read all the literature, and even spoken to a few people who had gone through the same thing. But nothing could prepare me for what lay ahead. It was the day after the surgery that my nightmare began.

The day after my surgery was torture. After popping a handful of Percocet pills, I became comfortably numb, but not as good as when the venomous snake called Dilaudid infiltrated my veins and my brain. The next few days were a blur, with me consuming Percocet like popcorn kernels. In no time, the bottle of Percocet was almost empty. I called the doctor's office for a refill. When the nurse asked how many I'd taken, I said two every four hours, just as the instructions said. To this day, I can't believe she accepted that answer.

The nurse responded with, "It says AS NEEDED for pain, and I said emphatically, "I've been in a lot of pain! Please have the doctor call in a refill". The nurse acknowledged my request and asked me to hold on. After ten minutes, she returned to the telephone line and posed the all-important question: "Which Pharmacy would you like to use"? They tempted me to say whatever was nearest my house, but I gave her the same place where I'd picked up my first prescription. She told me it should be ready in about an hour, and I silently cheered, mentally turning over an hourglass in my mind so I could start counting down.

I slowly descended the stairs and told my dad I needed a refill of my pain medication. Looking back now, I can't help but find it humorous that his response mirrored the nurses: "You have already taken an entire bottle of pills!" Calling to mind all my past feats while going after narcotic prescriptions, I replied yes, grabbed the car keys, and drove to what some might call the land of Oz, the pharmacy. As always, I was punctual. When I got there, I informed the girl behind the counter that my doctor had called in a prescription for me. The pharmacy tech asked for my name and typed it into her computer. To my horror, the pharmacy tech reported that nothing under my name was available. My stomach lurched as the last four Percocets wore off. Panic filled me as a million thoughts raced through my head about how I could get more pills without returning home empty-handed.

I need that feeling of joy again, and I've promised to wean off them after this bottle is gone. It's a promise I've made to myself for nearly 15 years. My mind tells me differently whenever I'm in the throes of it. That's how easy it is to deceive yourself when you're addicted. But it never happens, no matter how badly I want to believe it. "Let me ask the Pharmacist in the back," the young woman said. The woman's expression was showing me that she saw my desperation. I tried to catch some of their conversation as she left but could only make out a word or two. As soon as she returned from the back room, where all the medicine was kept, I felt my heart race faster, and my panic about finding more intensified.

The pharmacist told me they would fill the order in around an hour. A damn hour, are you kidding me? Why an hour? I internally groaned with annoyance. 'What must he do when filling a prescription only takes one step?" The more rational part of my mind told me I had to wait, so I sat in the chair.

Meanwhile, the euphoria from the Percocet I had taken three hours ago had worn off, and now I felt a wave of depression come over me. I was desperate for another dose that would make everything excellent again, but it seemed like days before the young lady returned with a small white bag containing what would help me feel better in half an hour. "Your prescription is ready, Mr Powers," she said, and with that, my outlook shifted. I nodded, took out another twenty-dollar bill, and paid the entrance fee to ride this emotionally charged rollercoaster again. When I turned away from the door, my hands were already tearing away the paper bag that held the bottle of the dream-making demons.

As I opened it, I was delighted that the doctor had prescribed me a whopping sixty tablets! It felt like fireworks going off in my head - great! These sixty tablets would keep me going for weeks until I finally quit these damn pills. This was probably the second millionth time my brain made this promise to quit during the fifteen years I spent addicted to painkillers, yet I believed it every single time. When I returned home, the euphoria peaked, and my mind whispered, "It'll be alright, Jimmy, don't worry; be happy!" A week went by in a blur. Finally, suitcase packed, I headed back home to my wife and children.

"Never to suffer would never to have been blessed"

Edgar Allen Poe

Chapter 7

Daddy's Home

☐   You're likely thinking about why I went to my dad's house when I married and had two small kids. Our marriage was deteriorating rapidly before my injury, so my wife had no desire to take care of me while I was convalescing at home. We figured it would be best to stay with my father for the initial recovery period. Plus, with two children aged 3 and 5 and a 100 lb golden retriever running around, it made more sense than trying to make do at our house. This chapter won't be long since we didn't stay long there! After a couple of weeks of recuperating while on painkillers, we both agreed that divorce was the best solution. As I'm writing this, it all feels like a blur.

One day, feeling the effects of a potent narcotic, I gathered my belongings and rented an apartment. As I write this chapter, I can't help but wonder if I would have made such a decision sober. The drug-induced logic of 'everything will be just fine' was surely false reassurance from the devil—the master of deceit, and narcotics being his best friend. They did not coerce me into taking these drugs that had control over me for fifteen years. It's a thought-provoking comparison: is it more dangerous to have a loaded 357 magnum pointed at your temple or constantly hold a bottle of Percocet? The former brings instant death, while the latter slowly sucks one down in an ever-spinning spiral.

Drug addiction takes away so much from you; it robs you of your time, pulls away your ambition, and destroys your relationships. The pursuit of drugs has taken the place of quality time with family and friends, as well as personal growth. It's an endless cycle: the more time spent searching for a fix, the less time spent enjoying life or making progress. Your insatiable hunger for opiates has replaced the ambition and drive that used to fuel your passion for life. Nothing else matters anymore–not school, work, or hobbies– nothing can compete with the pull of opiates and the instant gratification they provide. All energy is directed towards getting high, leaving no room for ambition. Drug addiction destroys relationships by creating a divide between oneself and loved ones. Friendships become strained as loved ones begin slowly pulling away. The devil is the master of deceit, that's for damn sure, and narcotics are his best lure! He held my hand and walked with me for 15 years, constantly reminding me, "Don't worry, Jimmy, everything will be fine"!

This chapter is brief because my return home was short-lived as well. My drug-addled brain convinced me that leaving my family was the right decision. There was no looking back after I put that train in motion. A decision that still affects my life today.

" Solitude was my only consolation- deep, dark, solitude."

Mary Shelley

Chapter 8

My First Rodeo

☐   About a week later, I moved into my new apartment with my

fifth bottle of Percocet, nearly empty. My high brain waves

convinced me that everything was okay. I peered down at the bottle and saw five pills left. My usual dose was six; would five suffice? Some people believe we are living in hell on earth, but for me, hell was hitting the bottom of a prescription container filled only with air when no more pills remained inside; when they were gone, so was the genie from the bottle. Not when there are one or two pills left, but when there is nothing but fucking air between your fingers and the bottom of the empty bottle which a few days ago held the genie in the bottle I loved. They made dreams of the things that continuously told me that all were just fine and dandy! I think every human being has an addiction of some variety. Like when some people say, "he has an addictive personality. Shit, I have an addictive personality.

The first time I took one of those magic little pills, I was hooked. Even after all these years, I still wonder how something so small could make me feel so powerful and invincible. If only someone had warned me what this would lead to–taking control of my mind, body, and soul. I've seen people possessed by the devil who have needed an exorcism from a Catholic priest.

It would have been as easy as calling a priest and having a couple-hour exorcism! But I eventually realized that pill addiction is much harder to get rid of: no matter how hard I tried, it seemed like I could never fully get rid of it.

I could beat the addicted demon inside of me. I would have to be very careful and methodical in my actions, focusing all of my energy on stopping the cravings before they could even begin. Slow and steady would win this race and keep me safe from harm. It would take time for me to heal, but what was time except for a way to measure one's progress? There was no actual meaning behind it, only the context it gave each day so that you knew how far you'd come since you began and where you were going. I sat in the darkness alone, cursing at myself, letting my mind rage against itself as I tried to find a way out of my cage. Like a rat nibbling on cheese, I clawed at the walls of my cell, waiting for a chance to escape, only to find myself stuck in the most minor corner of my mind. Unlike the rat trapped by logical contraptions of death, I wished for no release, wishing instead to remain there forever until my body died without me. I would come to find out you can never fully exercise this beast.

I could beat him slowly but surely, though, and put him in that deep, dark, dank hole with chains on his hooves!

I wish the pharmacist had warned me of the throes of agony I would soon endure after taking my prescription. Those pills brought me a sense of euphoria like nothing else ever had before. They said to take it as needed for pain, but it provided so much more than comfort. What started as simply trying to feel better became a 15-year-long living hell. If only I had known, maybe I wouldn't have taken them. I hope someone will read this and reconsider taking this same roller coaster ride if they're on the verge of hopping into the line. I know from experience that a good idea must be far away. So run! Run as fast and as far away from these drugs before it is too late.

Oops, I'm rambling again, back to my hell. I had been in my new apartment for a week and stopped taking the Percocet after this bottle was gone. So I took the last five tablets at around 5 pm and started riding the Percocet pony at about 6.

. Sitting on my patio that evening, feeling all was right with the world, I went to bed at 10, convinced that tomorrow would be a better day without relying on Percocet. However, when I woke up at 3 am to use the bathroom, I realized something wasn't quite right. I took a leak and fell back to sleep.

I felt discomfort when I awoke at 10 am, and my mind said, 'Oh no! I'm out of pills. My brain repeated the same thought, like an old vinyl record player with the needle stuck. This mental loop kept spinning until it had me near panic level. Then, I felt a pain in my neck. My brain remarked, "I told you that you would need more!" referring to pills. So, I lay back down and tried sleeping. When I did, I had the first of many nightmares that would haunt me for the next fifteen years.

The dream was always the same. I was on an airplane, and it was going to crash. Everything felt so real! As I peered out of the window, I could see the ground coming closer and closer. Then, suddenly, there was a loud screeching sound as the wing snapped off. It almost sounded like thousands of people dragging their nails on a chalkboard at max volume. Everyone started screaming and crying, and right before impact, there was a tremendous boom. Something suddenly transported my mind and body to a jet hangar filled with caskets from floor to ceiling. Everywhere I looked, the coffins were open and drenched in blood. There were some victims missing limbs, or half of the head or entire heads or torsos were gone.

As I stumbled into the hangar, my steps became shaky. It felt like I was walking in a bowl of half-set jello. I looked down to find it full of body parts tangled in an eerie network of arteries and veins. Jet fuel and a pungent odor of burnt flesh were in the air. Even now, this metallic, putrid scent lingers in my nostrils when I have a dream. It is always the same nightmarish vision; has this been a foreshadowing of what would come if I continued with my addiction to pills? This recurring dream haunted me the entire time. Does this recurring nightmare have a connection to my addiction? Was my unconscious mind cautioning me about the dangerous situation I was in?

When I awoke around 3 pm, I felt awful. Headache, nausea, and profuse sweating had all taken hold of me. My mind told me to call the doctor and get a refill, but this was after his office told me it would be the last one they'd be allowing. "Fuck it," my thoughts said. Before I could follow through on the command, it seized me with intense stomach pains that sent me sprinting to the bathroom, where I experienced the worst diarrhea of my life. It was like there was an imaginary firefighter inside me who was squirting water out of my ass to snuff out whatever flames were burning at the bottom of the bowl. As this figure worked his magic, sweat began pouring from my forehead so hard it nearly stung as it escaped through my pores. By then, my stomach had emptied itself of everything within.

My brain was screaming at me to call the doctor's office. I started dialing, then stopped, questioning myself. Come on, it demanded, call the damn doctor and get a refill! I dialed once more and soon heard someone answer. I politely explained my situation: I had undergone neck surgery with Dr. Smith and now needed a refill on my medication. Anxiety rose within me as I waited for an answer; what would I do if they said no? My stomach felt cramped as sweat pooled on my forehead. Finally, she came back on the telephone line.

"Mr. Powers, the doctor, had informed me you shouldn't be in this much pain, and he won't be able to call in a refill for my pain medication.". Complete panic washed over me as soon as I heard those words, and it continued down my body until it reached my toes! My entire being was in complete panic mode! It was all I could do to make it to the bathroom before the mini-firefighter started shooting everything out of my body again with his little hose! It was now around 5 pm. I felt incredibly down for the first time in my life. My mind was still screaming for me to get more pills. If only I could sleep until tomorrow, maybe I'd feel better.

I scoured my cupboards and found a bottle of unused Nyquil. Perfect, I thought and threw off the dosing cap before downing half the contents in one swallow. I must have dozed off as I awoke at midnight feeling worse than ever. I had drenched my bed with sweat and felt like my skin was on fire. No matter how hard I scratched, I couldn't soothe the itch. The little firefighter that lived within me had returned, flooding my insides with his hose. As I rushed to the bathroom, all I could think was, how can I get more pills to end this torture?

I tried to get up to crawl back into bed, but my stomach was in knots, so I vomited yellow acidic bile all over the bathroom tiles. This was the first time I ever experienced withdrawal from pills and not the last. An incessant song kept playing in my mind: "You have to get more pills! GET MORE PILLS! GET MORE PILLS!" Could I be going insane? This process of getting off them twisted my thoughts. It was some powerful stuff! I started referring to this entire experience as "Riding the Bull," like how I'd imagine your body would feel after riding an actual bull. My first ride wasn't pleasant, and I never wanted to get on again. To forget what was happening, I drank the other half of the bottle of Nyquil and somehow fell asleep, even though the little monster in my brain still kept insisting that I should try to get more pills in any way possible. Would I ride the bull again? Would this be my first and last rodeo?

" If you can quit for a day, you can quit for a lifetime"

Benjamin Alire Sáenz

Chapter 9

The Ride Has Just Begun

The next day, I awoke to a toxic smell and realized I was lying in an inch of my stinking sweat. The odor was reminiscent of rotting fruit, and it permeated the room. As I tried to crawl out of bed, I felt something wet and sticky on my rear end and underwear, which turned out not to be what I thought it was. After peeking down my boxers, I realized that my buddy, the firefighter, must have paid me another visit while I slept off a bottle of Nyquil from the day before. No, it wasn't sweat. I had shit the bed! Someone must have dumped a murky, viscous water bucket filled with excrement over me. It saturated my bed with bodily fluids from seemingly every outlet. "Dear Lord," I thought as I stood there stunned, looking at my beloved king-size bed I had practically destroyed.

I stumbled into the shower and turned on the hot water. It felt like a million tiny stings as I stood beneath the spray. "Damn," I thought to myself, "it even hurts to take a shower." I grudgingly finished cleaning off all the internal and external body fluids from my skin, including having to scrape dried-up gunk from the backs of my calves. I dried off with what felt like coarse sandpaper when I finished.

Withdrawing, I knew the feelings of desperation and hopelessness that swallowed me whole like a giant wave. Even the most luxurious item I had, the plush towel from HomeGoods, couldn't stop my pain. Anything to control these feelings was necessary! Exhausted from trying to clean off the mess, I wondered why on earth I hadn't bought that moisture-resistant mattress cover when I was linen shopping! Finally cleaned up, I was determined to make this feeling disappear by any means possible. Immediately, I called a friend who used pills. My brain screamed out for relief, refusing to accept tomorrow would be better without pills - not even close! In a matter of moments, the prescription bottle was empty, and my worries dissolved with each pill ingested.

I would realize in the following years that tomorrow never comes. Following this realization, I heard a tired voice from the other end of my phone call with my buddy. "Hey bro, what's going on?" I asked after he answered. "Not much," he replied sluggishly. "You know where I can get some pain pills? Like Percocet or something?" I inquired casually as if I were asking for a cheeseburger from McDonald's drive-thru. "How many are you looking for?" he inquisitively wondered. I heard an inquiry around ten thousand times in the next fifteen years - "How many do you have?". "How much are they?" I followed up as assurance swept over me. He assured me he had 10 mg Lortabs available for five bucks each; when I asked if it was like a 10mg Percocet, he promptly responded with a yes. This conversation marked my first introduction to hydrocodone or Lortabs.

That's fine," I replied, my mind already beginning to scream another question: "When can I get them?" "You can start heading this way," he responded. The little monster in my head said: "He already had it when you called." "Yippie yi yay!" my brain replied. Let me explain how these petty demons of the mind can mess with a person. I could be in a complete state of panic and physical withdrawal–only to hear I was getting pills within a minute or hours, and suddenly, this enormous wave of adrenaline and dopamine would take over my senses. That's why it's called a mind fuck, right? The blind placebo tests are one hundred percent precise. At least they were for me. I hopped in my car and made my five-mile journey that no longer seemed impossible! As I sat in traffic at a red light, the little monster in my brain thought up a joke, and I laughed uncontrollably. It was like: "They should make an express lane for people going to get their drugs, one that has no speed limits, traffic jams, or stop lights!" My internal joke sent me into another fit of laughter as I stepped on the gas pedal like a drag racer, leaving the starting line when the light turned green.

I greeted my friend when he opened the door. He seemed to feel worse than I did. He handed me a bag of pills that were light sky blue, something I'd never seen before. As I retrieved six hundred-dollar bills from my pocket, I asked if they would do the same thing as 10mg of Percocet. He replied affirmatively. But then the little monster in my head demanded I take seven rather than the six I had planned. So I used my friend's restroom. "An extra pill won't hurt me, right?" My irrational mind piped up again. I quickly swallowed seven pills and left with a massive smile on my face.

As I walked out of my friend's apartment, the weight of negativity crashed onto me like a ton of bricks. All the past mistakes and bad choices came rushing to my mind like a storm surge. Questions flooded my thoughts: what was I going to do now? I had left my family, and all I had in my account was around two grand (half of which was already gone because I told my wife I would pay for the children monthly). My whole mind felt like it was sinking into a negative abyss, unable to come up for air. In all my years on this planet, I had never navigated through such an abysmal amount of negative thoughts before.

All my life, I had always looked at the glass as half full. But here I was, sitting at a traffic light, ready to break down and cry. That's when the little monster in my head told me not to worry because I had taken something to make it all disappear. "Man up," it said, "You big pussy!" I headed to the dollar store, hoping to find cheap cleaning supplies. Just as I walked into the shop, the fire alarm suddenly sounded. My inner firefighter shouted for me to run to the restroom before he turned on his hose! With no time to spare, I clutched my stomach and sprinted to the bathroom. After five minutes of intense discomfort, I emerged from the stall and set off to get supplies to sanitize my apartment. I tumbled out of the bathroom and began my quest to cleanse my apartment.

The warmth of the drug that had become so familiar to me in such a short time spread from my head to my toes. "See, Jimmy, everything is going to be okay!" said the little monster softly. All the negative thoughts plaguing me for the last 24 hours were gone, replaced by unicorns and rainbows. "Just keep feeding me regularly, and life will be full of your favorite treats. Oh, and don't worry, I will always let you know when it's time for more.", he said, laughing. After spending most of what I had left of my money on cleaning supplies, I floated back to my car, feeling like nothing could or would go wrong. It was the same feeling I had as a child on Christmas Eve, a warm love. Wow, I want to feel this good all the time! I thought as I drove away. Keep this term in mind, Mindfuck, because these pills and that little monster inside your head will always make you think life is perfect every time that slow drip of

narcotics seeps into your bloodstream. It always whispers, "Don't

worry, Be Happy!".

" Curiosity is gluttony, to see is to devour."

Victor Hugo

Chapter 10

Mr. Clean and His Trip To The Moon

I returned to my apartment and started cleaning. I was

cleaning like a madman, cranking up the AC/DC and scrubbing the entire apartment from front to back. I also purchased a box of baking soda and poured the entire contents over my mattress. I had heard this would draw the moisture or shit water out of my bed. An hour later, I vacuumed it up, and it reduced the shit water moisture content in my mattress almost to none. I plugged in a couple of glades scent plugins and sat down to admire the cleanliness of my lil' piece of heaven, where I could be myself and do what the fuck I wanted to and when.

I missed my children, but damn sure not my wife! It was about seven o'clock in the evening, and my appetite had returned, and I ordered some Chinese delivery. As I dialed the order in, that little monster in my head came to life again and said, "Hey, I'm not feeling as well as I was a little while ago. You need to feed me before yourself because those pills work better on an empty stomach."

I agreed with him, went to my closet, and pulled out the baggie of Lortab, which now contained 93 tablets, or should I now say held 86 tablets. I ordered the food, sat on the couch, and waited. Blastoff occurred about 45 minutes after the seven tablets began slithering their way through my stomach, small intestines, and liver, finally delivering that burst of sunshine and good euphoric rush feeling to my brain in which the little monster lived.

A line from the song Rocket Man by Elton John came into my head: "I'm not the man they think I am at home, oh no, no, no, I'm a rocket man." About this time, the doorbell rang, and it was time to fuck up this General Tao's chicken and fried dumplings I had ordered. I noticed I was starving and had eaten nothing in about 30 hours. I honestly, now, as I look back, don't remember a lot about the week that followed. The only thing I remember vividly is that less than a week later, my once-full baggie of 100 Lortab was down to the last few, and the little monster was getting restless!

" Complete abstinence is easier than perfect moderation."

St. Augustine

Chapter 11

Lawyers, Guns and Money

I returned to my apartment and started cleaning. I was cleaning like a madman, cranking up the AC/DC and scrubbing the entire apartment from front to back. I also purchased a box of baking soda and poured the entire contents over my mattress. I had heard this would draw the moisture or shit water out of my bed. An hour later, I vacuumed it up, and it reduced the shit water moisture content in my mattress almost to none. I plugged in a couple of glades scent plugins and sat down to admire the cleanliness of my lil' piece of heaven, where I could be myself and do what the fuck I wanted to and when.

I missed my children, but damn sure not my wife! It was about seven o'clock in the evening, and my appetite had returned, and I ordered some Chinese delivery. As I dialed the order in, that little monster in my head came to life again and said, "Hey, I'm not feeling as well as I was a little while ago. You need to feed me before yourself because those pills work better on an empty stomach."

I agreed with him, went to my closet, and pulled out the baggie of Lortab, which now contained ninety-three or eighty-six tablets. I ordered the food, sat on the couch, and waited. Blastoff

occurred about forty-five minutes after the seven tablets began

slithering their way through my stomach, small intestines, and liver,

finally delivering that burst of sunshine and good euphoric rush

feeling to my brain in which the little monster lived.

A line from the song Rocket Man by Elton John came into

my head: "I'm not the man they think I am at home, oh no, no, no,

I'm a rocket man." About this time, the doorbell rang, and it was

time to fuck up this General Tao's chicken and fried dumplings I had

ordered. I noticed I was starving and had eaten nothing in about

thirty hours. I honestly, now, as I look back, don't remember a lot

about the week that followed. The only thing I remember vividly is

that less than a week later, my once-full baggie of one hundred

Lortab was down to the last few, and the little monster was getting

restless!

" The Devil's voice is sweet to hear"

Stephen King

Chapter 12

Well, How Did I Get Here?

The weeks flew by like a warm summer breeze. I took my daily dose of seven Lortabs three times a day. My intake was 210 mg of hydrocodone daily, with 325 mg of acetaminophen or aspirin accompanying each 10mg pill. It was a massive amount for my liver and kidneys to process, but I kept the monster in his shit-filled cage. I fed the lil monster, kept him silent, and locked him away. I remembered my daughters visiting my apartment for the first time on Friday afternoon. I felt strange, numb from the uncertainty of their reaction. The weekend went better than expected; they were young enough to find joy in anything and everything around them. Unbeknownst to them, their father was in the throes of a dark addiction that threatened to consume his mind, heart, and soul. It had already destroyed their Norman Rockwellesque idyllic childhood. Now, at 30 and 31, they still despise me to this day for the wrongs I have done. I carry that with me to this day and wonder if I will ever have a relationship with my daughters, see my grandchildren, and be a part of their lives again.

My answer was to buy my daughters some paints and allow them to decorate the walls in their new bedroom. "Go Nuts!" I said with a big smile on my face. "This is your home away from home!". We could still laugh and act like nothing was wrong despite the recent changes in our lives. If only things could be that easy now.

I returned to my apartment on Sunday night in a deep depression. I reached into my closet and pulled out my nearly empty bag of Lortabs, spilling them onto the bed. Eleven pills remained. My drug-addled brain began calculating how many I should take: six now, five in the morning? Or maybe seven now and four in the morning? Before I could decide, I called my buddy, Ben, and found he could get me another hundred by noon tomorrow. The lil monster inside of me shouted, "Fuck it! We can get more later; take them all now!" The rational side argued that the most I'd ever taken at once was seven, so taking all eleven wasn't a good idea. As usual, the little monster in my head. I won out in the end. I soon discovered that my inner voice was a formidable opponent. It never lost an argument. So, I took eleven blue Lortab tablets and lit up a cigarette as I waited for the effects to kick in. After about half an hour, all the intense feelings of depression had vanished, and the little monster inside was caroling his favorite tune, "Don't Worry, Be Happy!". Suddenly, everything seemed alright. The cigarette butt-filled ashtray on my patio served as a reminder of what had just happened, and I went back into my room to take a shower.

The first thing I noticed when I stepped into my room to shower was the empty baggie, and a wave of panic hit me: I had run out of pills. But I was still feeling a slight buzz from the 110 milligrams of hydrocodone I had taken earlier, and that brought the thought of how good it would be to get the full baggy back in 13 hours. The hot water felt like a protective cocoon as it slid down my body. "Everything will be okay.", I reassured myself. Captain Hydrocodone had taken over the train, and it seemed to move along just fine. After gobbling down a frozen pizza and smoking another Marlboro Light, I tried to sleep but couldn't drift off. This insomnia hadn't happened before; usually, sleeping came quickly to me.

During my days as a person with an addiction, I learned that high-dose narcotics coursing through your veins could make it hard to sleep, especially if you'd taken a lot of them. Eventually, after hours of lying there, I drifted off into dreamland. My usual nightmare returned: the same airplane doing its death spiral dive, followed by me trudging knee-deep through body fluid and dismembered corpses in the hangar full of caskets and dead people. It was ending inevitably in the same way the nightmare always did.

As soon as I awoke from my ten am10 am slumber, the little monster in my head screamed that I didn't have any pills. He kept repeating it until he finished with a demand to get some pills or else. I grabbed the phone and dialed my buddy, Ben, but the call went unanswered. "Get me some fucking pills and feed me now!". I grabbed the phone, punched in my friend's number, and waited as it rang out. It seemed forever before it stopped ringing, sending my brain into panic. My mind raced with fear as I looked at the giant bull waiting for me to enter the chute and take my turn on a sweaty, shaking, and vomiting ride.

"Jesus, I don't want to go through that again.", I thought. My still sober mind was begging me not to have to go through this again. I was trembling with panic, and it made me nauseous to even think about the possibility that he might not answer. I picked up my phone and dialed again, and luckily, his groggy voice said, "Hello?" in response. "What's up, brother?" I asked as calmly as possible. He muttered nonchalantly, "Nothin' much, still sleeping. The little monster inside my head shouted: "WELL, GET THE FUCK UP!". Ben did not hear the lil monster's demand and continued to speak casually, "I forgot to call you back yesterday and tell you my buddy is out of town.". When do you think you will hook me up?" I asked calmly. "I don't know," he answered, prompting a flurry of angry screaming from the lil monster.

"I will contact you if I find any," he said. Cold sweat filled my forehead, and I could feel my stomach cramping before the conversation ended. The withdrawal rodeo was pulling into town, and I was first up in the bull riding event. "FUCK"! I thought as I hung up the phone and spent the rest of the day pacing between my couch and bed. My physical and mental state were in complete chaos and panic. The rodeo was in town, and I was in the bull's grasp and fury! Every orifice of my body spilled out of fluids. It was a depressing time for me, one which had me so close to suicide that it scared me.

At around 8 pm, my madness kicked in, and my inventive brain came up with the idea that I would later cherish whenever the metaphorical rodeo was in town and I couldn't get my pills in the usual way. As a poker player says, this was my ace in the hole.

" The Rodeo ain't over until the bull riders ride."

Ralph Carpenter

Chapter 13

"911, what's your emergency?"

Around eleven o'clock, my stomach began cramping unbearably, and my mind felt scattered. The little monster's voice that I'd grown so accustomed to when I was high had changed: it went from friendly and understanding to spiteful, as I was no longer under the influence of drugs. "What in the world am I going to do?" the voice shook me out of it. All I wanted was one of those Dilaudid shots to flow through my veins like before.

I recalled my buddy saying how painful it had been to have kidney stones. The nurses at the hospital had told him it was the worst agony a man could experience compared to a woman giving birth. Then, an idea struck me: this would be the perfect way to get out of this brutal withdrawal state and get back on the narcotic express!

Without more ado, I sat on the toilet and let the familiar burning sensation of Tabasco sauce course through me. I wrapped up hastily, wearing shorts and a t-shirt, before driving off for my first phony emergency room appointment. For the following fifteen years, I visited around one hundred or even one hundred fifty E.R.s in different states without health insurance. I'd always leave my insurance card at home when I saw the emergency room, which never stopped me from getting the needed care. My actions were irresponsible and have likely contributed to why healthcare is so expensive today - to which I apologize.

That day, I skidded into the emergency parking lot, jumped out of the car, and put on a show worthy of an Academy Award. Holding my side and nearly doubled over in pain, I cried out for help. The nurse asked me where it hurt, and as if inspired by my performance, I fell to one knee and said that a butcher knife was stabbing me in my side. "Please get it out!". I could have beaten out

Laurence Olivier with my Oscar-winning performance. I moaned groaned, and made it incredibly awkward for everyone involved.

A nurse materialized from behind the automatic doors, rolling a wheelchair, and they immediately took me to an E.R. room with no questions asked. She told another nurse, "I believe he has kidney stones," as they helped me onto the hospital bed. Then, this new nurse swabbed my forearm with an alcohol swab and asked if I had any allergies to medications. After being told I wasn't allergic to anything, she said she would put me in an intravenous line to give me some pain relief. Suddenly, the song "Tell Me Something Good" flooded my mind, and it took me a few seconds to process what she had just said. Could it be possible that she was going to give me the drug Dilaudid?

I felt an instant surge of energy when the nurse walked over with two syringes full of "magic juice." My mind lit up like fireworks, and the little monster in my head started dancing happily. The nurse said, "The first one is called Phenergan. This will help you with the nausea from the narcotics. The second medication is Dilaudid. This will help you with your pain." I anxiously watched as she inserted the second needle into my I.V. snake. Suddenly, a wave of warmth surged through my veins and arteries and hit my dopamine receptors—it was like winning the jackpot! In my mind's eye, I could almost see Chef Emeril Lagasse throwing in some cayenne pepper while shouting "BAM!" which perfectly described what it felt like.

The nurse returned with my punched ticket for the Dilaudid Express: Bam! In less than five seconds after she injected the pain reliever into my vein, I felt utterly relieved from my withdrawal symptoms. I had an incredible sensation of invincibility that nothing else mattered. 'Tell Me Something Good' cheerfully played in my head once

After singing along to Rufus in my head for a few minutes, the nurse asked me how I felt. I told her it was better but still quite painful. She inquired what the intensity of the pain was when I arrived, to which I said ten out of ten. She asked what it was now; remembering to be careful with my words, I replied with an eight. The little monster reminded me that there was still a stabbing sensation despite the decrease in sharpness. Upon hearing this, she said she'd get more medication. Bingo!

The little monster inside me did the happy dance. I questioned, "Will I truly receive more Dilaudid?" A few minutes later, a second dose of Dilaudid made its way into my veins and rushed directly to my dopamine center. The ecstasy that followed was extraordinary. The nurse returned to check my vitals, knocking me out of my euphoric state. I said I'd recovered; the little monster shouted for more. With haste, I asked for another shot to appease him. She said she'd have to get permission from the doctor first. "Hurry!" he added.

I cursed in my head. Have the people at the hospital noticed? Have I been too greedy, asking for one more shot? Will they take all my medication away? I tried just to enjoy the feeling, rocking back and forth, thinking that maybe if I could last long enough, I could quit tomorrow. Time seemed to slow until the nurse finally returned with one more shot of Dilaudid. Everything calmed down, but the little voice inside me urged me on. The nurse also said I might need some scans so they could find out where the kidney stones were chilling.

My rational brain chimed in that there might be a slight problem with producing an actual kidney stone. I was going to have to give another performance of a lifetime. As always, my inner Lawrence Olivier was ready to aid me when I needed a quick answer. "I'm allergic to dye, ma'am," I said, trying not to let my voice slur or giggle. "Okay," she replied. A few minutes later, she came back with a cup-like object—the doctor wanted me to urinate into it so they could examine and identify any stones that might pass through. She instructed me to drink plenty of fluids—especially cranberry juice. "Okay, sounds good, and I will," I promised her. "I'll be back in a few minutes with your discharge papers, and you can go home. Oh, did you drive, or did someone drop you off?"

Quickly, thinking kicked in; I lied and told the nurse that my friend was returning to pick me up. The nurse had reassured me that driving was not an option. I agreed with her and appeased any concern with a trustworthy smile. Afterward, I couldn't help but ponder what would happen if I tried to leave the E.R. in a vehicle. Would they physically try to stop me?

The lil monster shouted obscenities as I imagined hopping into my car like an outlaw. "Fuck 'em, fuck 'em all!". The little monster in my head was giving everyone the bird as we peeled out of the imaginary parking lot in front of all the fictional people who watched in awe. "FUCK EM!" This was becoming the little monster's favorite line, and he would use it over and over in the next 15 years to come.

The nurse returned shortly with my release forms and a prescription for 10 Percocet. It tempted me to cry out, "WTF!?!" at the number, but I silenced it with the reason that ten pills were better than none. We quietly exited the E.R. doors, scanning the area for potential watchers, only to realize they had no power over me anyway. I got into the car and drove home, my brain still suspended in the ether.

" Pleasure and Erotica are on the menu today, because we might not eat tomorrow."

James Powers

Chapter 14

Hello, I Love You. Won't You Tell Me Your Name

When I woke up the next day, my head felt full of cotton. I lay still in bed for half an hour, reliving the events inside the emergency room from the previous night. It had been such a simple way to get high - especially when I'd run out of pills and was going through withdrawal. I pulled off my plan without a hitch. My mind cackled at how smoothly it had gone, and I smiled in bed. Then I noticed the prescription paper beside me with orders from the doctor for 10 Percocet. But the lil monster inside my brain proposed adding a 0 to make that number 100. The rational part of my mind quickly realized that no E.R. doctor would prescribe a hundred pills, so I felt grateful that I had squashed the awful idea. I slowly got out of bed and walked to the bathroom to pee, then went into my living room and sat down. I fought the urge to go into withdrawal as I thought of having to get on that nasty bull in its pen of projectile vomiting and cold sweats. So, I put my clothes on and headed to the Walgreens, where I'd filled prescriptions. The young lady behind the counter told me it would be ready in around 30 minutes. I said that was fine and I'd wander around until it was ready. I was making my presence known, which usually worked, giving them an extra urge to hurry and fill the prescription faster while I was waiting there. That, plus just sitting in a chair where people stay and staring them down, made them fill prescriptions faster. At least, those were my theories.

The young woman behind the counter announced, "Mr. Powers, your prescription is ready." I had hovered around them for so long that it took less time than they had said. "Thanks," I muttered, paying for the pills before leaving the pharmacy. On my way home, the lil monster kept demanding that I make a detour to purchase a Coke and down all 10 of the pills I had just filled. "I'm hungry, motherfucker," my monster shouted ad nauseam until I arrived back at my apartment. As soon as I entered, I quickly gulped down the ten Percocets I had just bought from Walgreens. My demons were silenced and disappeared into his cave to prepare for lift-off.

In a matter of minutes, the rush of pleasure I had grown to love coursed through my body. However, something was different this time; it didn't feel as good as usual. I reasoned it must have been because of the high dose of Dilaudid I received at the hospital last night. The Percocets didn't have the same strength as the intravenous medication I received, but it was still something to prevent withdrawal. The thought of withdrawal ignited a fire inside me.

I grabbed my phone and dialed up my buddy. "Yo, what's up?" he said. "Nothing much. I was just about to call you. My guy's back if you need anything. The little monster got his dancing shoes on and started doing his version of the moonwalk! "I responded, "When can I come pick up 100? Right now, he said. "I knew you'd want them, so when he came by earlier today, I had him leave me 100 for you.". "GREAT!" be there in 30 minutes ", I answered without hesitation. I hopped in my car and drove straight to the nearest ATM, taking out a limit of 600 dollars before taking off like a lightning bolt and arriving at his house ahead of time.

"What in the hell, man? Did you sprout wings and fly here or something?" He joked as he opened his apartment door. "Nah, man, I don't mess around," I chuckled as I walked into his humble abode. "Listen, dude, I'm not making any money from these, so would it be alright if I just introduced you to him so you can deal with him directly?" Sure, that would be fine with me, "I assuredly replied. "Alrighty then; if you've got a few extra minutes here, let me call him right now—he lives in this very complex." "Fantastic!" I replied eagerly. He dialed the number, and the person on the line told us I could drop by immediately.'

"Ben told me you might be interested in some pills," he exclaimed. This was the first time I met Rick. Rick was, and I hope still is, a great standup human being who was selling his prescribed pain pills to make ends meet with his meager SSI benefits. His apartment was decorated with old but clean furniture that reminded me of my grandmother's house 20 years ago. He also looked exactly like Sergeant Carter from the old Gomer Pyle show. It must have been the flat top.

"Yeah, I have been buying a few from him, and he says he's not charging me for them," I replied with a laugh to break the tension in the room. "I need about 100 a week," I said. "I don't think I can give you that many every week," he answered. "Will you sell the entire prescription every month?" I asked. "Sure, no problem," He agreed. "Do you like pain pills? Lortabs?" he inquired. "Yes," I confirmed. "Ok," he said, offering to sell me all 120 for $5 each on the first of every month. In my mind, I shouted, "Hell yeah!" and thanked him graciously. "Got any other sort of pills?" I asked casually. He gestured for me to follow him to his kitchen. We sat down at his all-wooden antique kitchen table. Rick opened up the corner-bottom kitchen cabinet. You know, the big ones where you store large pots and pans? He pulled out this giant, prehistoric-looking, huge Lazy Susan. I remember thinking, how did he get that big ass thing in there in the first place? I asked him jokingly if he had won the pill lottery. Rick just laughed.

Rick responded by explaining his veteran status and how it had resulted in PTSD, as well as shrapnel dispersed throughout his body. "I understand," I said sympathetically. "It was a long war, and you're only getting $900 monthly from the government?" He nodded, then added he was selling the prescriptions to supplement his income. My morality kicked in, and I offered not to buy them all if he needed them. However, the little monster within me told me to "shut up and purchase the pills ."He always overruled my conscience, and I looked at the spinning display filled with dozens of bottles, ranging from muscle relaxants to antipsychotics, alphabetized, quite an impressive setup. I laughed to myself. He sat it in the middle of the table and spun the lazy Susan like a roulette wheel, and I laughed out loud.

As I examined all the substances in Rick's carousel of illicit drugs, I noticed he lacked any oxycodone or hydrocodone. "Do you have any other pain pills on here, Rick?" I asked, just in case I had missed something. "No, the Lortab is the only pain medication I get," he responded. I slowly stood up from my stooping position and said, "I guess I will call you at the beginning of each month and come pick them up." Rick chuckled, "No need; just plan on arriving at four o'clock on the first day of every month. I'm a creature of habit; I leave here at nine in the morning to go to the V.A. to get my medications, then come back home by two-thirty or three o'clock - like clockwork!" "Sounds good to me," I added with a lighthearted laugh. Before leaving, Rick asked me warily if I was a cop. "the farthest thing from one, my friend," I replied. "I break out in hives if I even see a police car. Rick chuckled.

" Guests, like fish, smell after three days."

Benjamin Franklin

Chapter 15

Knock, knock. Who's there?

☐   After I got back from Rick's with my stash of Lortab, the little monster in my head told me to take ten more pills. I went home, counted 10 of the new blue Lortab, took them down with some water, and then returned to the pool. I lay in the sun for what felt like an hour, but it had been four hours. The combination of the sun and narcotics was heavenly; it was a feeling I never wanted to end. I collected my towel and Dr Pepper and headed back to my apartment, where I ordered my favorite Chinese delivery food - which always tasted terrific when I was on narcotics - ate it when it arrived, turned on the TV, and settled in for the night... or so I thought.

The effects of the ten Loratab I took a few hours ago were wearing off, and my mind drifted into a dark abyss. I wondered how I had ended up in this two-bedroom apartment—where was my wife? Where were my daughters? Had I traded away my once-idyllic life for an addiction-driven nightmare? My inner thoughts raced non-stop until the lil monster screamed from his now open cage. "You have 90 Lortabs in your closet, you dumbass. Go get ten and forget about all this negative shit."

I went into the bedroom, counted out twelve pills, and prepared to put two back, but that same little voice told me to take them all to get an even higher high. I got myself a cold Dr Pepper and swallowed six pills at a time, twice over. Within half an hour, my worries faded away, replaced with the same mantra that spoke directly to my narcotic-saturated brain, "Everything will be just fine."

The hydrocodone had kicked in, and I felt like I was soaring. After taking 10 Percocet and 22 Lortab in 12 hours, I thought I was safe to enjoy the buzz. Until there came a knock at my door. It never occurred to me that someone might knock on my door at 9 p.m. on a Sunday, so I didn't initially recognize the figure outside. Looking back, I sure wish I hadn't opened that door, but I did open it. When I finally realized who the person on the other side of the door was, it felt almost as if I were looking into a mirror.

"What's up, brother?" my old golfing mate, Ben, asked me. His eyes were like giant black saucers. "Not much, man," I answered him. "Come in and have a seat," I said as we entered the living room. "So, what have you been up to?" I inquired casually. "I got into a big argument with my wife, and she told me to leave the house," he said, eyes on the floor. "Same story here," I replied. "Got sick of all the fighting and crap, so I left my family too." He nodded in agreement, and we both surveyed each other's tired, drug-addled eyes.

I asked Ben casually, "Where have you been staying, bro? When he replied, "I slept in my car last night," it surprised me. "You can stay here a couple of days until you figure out what you will do?" I blurted out. "Aw man, that would be great! Are you sure you don't mind?" Ben replied eagerly. "Not at all, bruh," I assured Ben. He quickly left to grab some things from his car and returned shortly after.

What I have failed to mention is the feeling of dread that came over me the minute I welcomed Ben into my life and home. I knew what kind of monster I had invited in, yet the effects of the 12 Lortab were still coursing through me, and my impaired brain said, "It's alright, don't worry." How could I have been so stupid? Just a few months prior, his brother had asked me to be part of an intervention for him, and he had already left his wife and kids because of his binges on crack cocaine. Yet here I was, asking this monster to stay in my apartment. I felt foolish as he entered, carrying a laundry basket and suitcase. I kept thinking, "What are you doing?!" Tremors ran throughout my body as I realized, "How idiotic could one man be?".

Even though I knew it was wrong, the pills overrode my better judgment, and the devil stepped into my apartment. Welcome to my personal living nightmare, day one! Ben lugged his laundry bag and suitcase into my spare bedroom, which my daughters had decorated just the weekend prior. As I write this book, I have vowed not to edit out any part, no matter how painful it is for me to relive them. People will never forget the huge mistakes I made, and even though I feel forgiven by a higher power, I don't think I will ever be able to forgive myself.

Once Ben put his things in the spare bedroom, he joined me again on the couch. "She doesn't understand me," he said with a sigh, trying to come to terms with what his drug-induced behavior had done to his family. I nodded in sympathy. "I know how you feel; my situation is similar."

"Do you want to get high?" Ben asked, my mind already clouded by the effects of previous substances. "Have you ever smoked crack?" Ben asked casually as if asking for a soda or something. "No," I responded. "But I'm willing to try." He told me we needed a 2-liter bottle, aluminum foil, and a pen. Then he added something strange: "And start saving all your cigarette ashes in one ashtray; we'll need them." I did not question him and gathered everything we needed for our creation - an abomination that must have been from Satan himself!

Never in my wildest dreams could I have foreseen the journey these innocent-looking items would take me on. I sat there, absolutely astonished, watching Ben assemble the contraption like a child assembling Lego pieces. His intense concentration, as if he were working on his second Nobel Prize, told me he was confident about this invention. We didn't exchange a word, but I couldn't help but think, 'What am I doing here on a Sunday night? I didn't realize the torture my mind, body, and soul were about to endure.

I watched Ben neatly divide a piece of crack into four even parts, something I was sure he had done thousands of times before. This time, however, I smiled to myself at his skill. He made an aluminum foil bowl and placed it on the lid opening of the two-liter bottle he would use to smoke from. Then, he inserted the hollowed pen into the side of the bottle to act as the stem. He then poked a small hole in the side to act as a carburetor. After filling it halfway with water, he completed his contraption as he lit the blue-orange flame on the bowl containing one-fourth of the candle wax-looking substance, which I could only guess was crack.

I couldn't help but laugh inwardly at how intently focused he was. Ben's eyes almost popped out of his head! The concentration required for such a simple task easily rivaled that of a brain surgeon. He held one finger over the carburetor while inhaling slowly.

A pop caught my attention, followed by the crackling sound of what I soon recognized as crack. Mesmerized, I watched as a dense yellowish smoke filled the half-full two-liter bottle to where I could no longer see through it. Then, he quickly lifted his finger off the carburetor and inhaled the contents in one massive breath. Ben's face started turning red and blue from holding his breath for so long. Just when I thought he might explode, he finally exhaled with barely any smoke residue! I couldn't help but laugh at this man's impressive technique. He then continued his Frankenstein-type surgery and put fresh ashes and another piece of crack on the aluminum foil bowl before saying, "Your turn."

I lifted the lighter to the crack pipe and dragged it until the crack melted away. We both laughed, even though I had promised myself I'd never smoke crack. Now that I had taken 32 pain pills, it seemed like the "narcotic monster" living in my head was controlling how I thought and acted. The BIC lighter lit the aluminum bowl, and I kept pulling on it as I watched the dense, yellowish demon smoke fill the bottle. Then he told me to take my finger off the carburetor, and when I did, all that smoky content rushed into my lungs.

Nothing happened at first, and then about 1.2 seconds later, a mighty rush of euphoria and adrenaline overwhelmed me. Thirty seconds prior, I was in a lazy river on a hydrocodone-induced high, content, relaxed, and feeling nothing but joy. Now, I felt like I was on a rocket ship to somewhere unknown, but I was still feeling the effects of the pain pills! My friend asked me, "Do you like it? The only words I could get out were, "Feels great!" It truly felt great at that moment.

Now, I can look back and see what I was doing, called "Speedballing."Most people reading this will know exactly what it entails. For those who don't, allow me to explain: "Speedballing" is a term used in the drug world for mixing two different drugs with different effects to achieve a higher buzz than either could provide on its own. Speedballing is incredibly dangerous, as your body tells your heart to do two other things simultaneously - slow down and speed up. The most common combination for speedballing is heroin and cocaine; however, I had opted for crack cocaine and hydrocodone instead. Although it was a milder version of the typical mixture, my heart still frantically asked, "What are you doing?" But the euphoric feeling felt far too good to ignore. Before I could say no, my euphoric mind companion had already started his next journey.

"How much for that stuff?" I innocently asked. "We can get a gram for a hundred," Ben answered. "How long will it last?" I inquired again. "That depends on how fast we smoke it," Ben laughed. I understood. "By the look of things, not long with you and I," I joked. We both chuckled. "Fuck it. How much is an ounce? About a grand, maybe twelve hundred at the most," he informed me. "Let's just get an ounce. Five or six hundred each, and we can have a big rock, yeah?"

I proposed. Ben agreed enthusiastically. If we pooled our money together, a golf-ball-sized rock was within reach. "I can't get that much out of the ATM right now," he said. "Fuck it, I'll get the first ounce and you grab the second one, deal?" I had more money than ever in my account, so paying for one was no problem. That sixty-six thousand didn't last too long, though! "Deal," he nodded.

Ben grabbed his car keys, and we headed to the shopping center about a half mile away so I could use the ATM before picking up our admission ticket to the stars. He grabbed his keys, and out the door we went. Looking back, what a fucking ride this would be!

"What goes up must come down. Spinnin' wheel got to go 'round. Talkin' 'bout your troubles its   a cryin' sin. Ride a painted pony, let the spinnin' wheel spin."

Blood, Sweat & Tears

Chapter 16

Welcome to the Jungle

☐ Jumping into Ben's car, we drove towards my favorite ATM. We hadn't thought about the 600-dollar daily limit until I tried to withdraw money from the machine. "How much shit can we get for 600?" I asked him. "Should be about half an ounce.", Ben replied. We then began our journey into a dark and unfamiliar part of town. Taking each turn off the road with caution, it felt like we were inching closer and closer to the Devil's lair. In my 33 years of living in this town, I had never ventured into this part of town, and I would soon enough know why. I asked if this was safe, and he chuckled and said they didn't like strangers in this area. My heart was pounding with anxiety as I realized I had driven myself into a potential war zone. I had only experienced fear four times before, but this was different because it involved a matter of life or death.

This area was scary-looking shit, with a bunch of dangerous zombie-like creatures roaming the streets. It reminded me of Michael Jackson's video thriller, except this shit was for real, and this wasn't any choreographed dance with a bunch of Hollywood dancers! This shit was real life, authentic, scary fuckin real, trust me! When you get to this stop sign, flash your lights on and off," my buddy said, "What the fuck?" I thought, but only responded with "Okay." After I flashed my lights off and on, within what seemed like a millisecond, one of the Thriller dancers knocked on my window and motioned me to roll it down. I just about floored it and wanted to get as far away from this current situation as I could, but again, my narcotic-soaked brain overrode my common sense, and I cautiously rolled the window down. "Wha chew want?" Those are the words I heard, and before my vocal cords could vibrate, my buddy replied, "How much is a half ounce of hard? I thought, what the hell is hard? I soon found out that hard cocaine was crack, and soft meant you wanted powder. You ain't cops, are you? "OH FUCK" my brain screamed at me. I prayed that my buddy could answer because my vocal cords felt like someone had hit them with liquid nitrogen, completely freezing them up. I silently prayed my buddy could answer. "Nah, man, my name is Ben, and this is my buddy, Jimmy. I'm good friends with Lucky. He usually comes by the crib, but we were close and just ran down real quick," Ben calmly explained. "Cool, cool," Thriller Man responded, "Go around the block and meet me back here in 5 minutes".

"Sounds like a plan," Ben said as we pulled away from the stop sign, also known as the crack drive-thru. As we drove away, I saw a police car headed our way from a side street. "Oh shit," Ben muttered under his breath. "Relax, just tell them you're lost if they pull us over.". I shot him a doubtful glance. "You think they'll believe that shit, right?" I retorted. "They've heard it all before.". I cursed to myself and wondered why we had even come down this way. "Look, just stay calm. We have nothing illegal with us, and most of the officers patrolling this area are on Lucky's payroll, anyway." Despite Ben's words, my heart rate was through the roof. "Okay," I said meekly, then followed his instructions to drive around the block again. When we returned to our original spot, something seemed different. It was almost like someone had used a loudspeaker to announce something was off.

In my head, the entire production crew of the Thriller sequel were all now in the street, their attention on us and the car full of white boys with at least $600 visible inside. My foot was ready to floor it out of there, but before I could, I heard a knock on the window, and Thriller Dancer Number 1 reappeared with a bag, dropping it into Ben's hand with a "here's a half z." Ben handed him six crisp one-hundred-dollar bills from the ATM we had just been to, and off we went. I drove slowly away as if leaving something behind. "Let's get the hell out of here!" I said as I sped up. "Turn left here," instructed Rick, and when I did, everything behind us lit up like a Christmas tree at Rockefeller Plaza at Christmas.

"Oh shit," said. "Don't pull over until I hide this stuff." My thoughts were chaotic as I heard the police officer's intercom system boom, instructing me to pull over. "Not yet," Ben said as I began slowing down. In front of me was a group of Thriller dancers in pure flight mode. If half of them weren't Olympic athletes, they must have been close! Carefully, I applied the brakes and pulled over on the side of the road. "Be cool," Ben said, but our fate seemingly sealed.

"Put your hands back on the wheel," the officer instructed as his partner retrieved Ben from the car's front seat and placed him in the back of the second police car behind us. "Do you know why I pulled you over?" he casually asked. "No sir," I meekly replied, my brain repeating, "You dumbass, you dumbass, you dumbass," over and over again. Then something unexpected happened: the 10 Lortab

I had taken before we drove took effect, injecting a wave of warmth and confidence into my veins. The Lortab may have given me enough of an edge to talk my way out of trouble. "Sorry, officer, I thought I came to a complete stop," I said nervously. "Can I see your license, registration, and insurance card, please?" he inquired. "Sure, here is my license, and the registration and insurance card are in the glove box; do you want me to get them?" Ben had shown me where to find them before we left, just in case we got pulled over.

I knew I should have taken this as a sign not to go, but I was already in the middle of it all. "Do it with your right hand only," the officer said. I complied and handed him what he asked for without missing a beat. He told me to keep my hands on the steering wheel until he returned. As I glanced at the rearview mirror, all I could see were those bright car headlights that lit up half of the street. I laughed as I thought of it, like the ending of a suspense movie—nobody was around. But then, dread overwhelmed me; what was Ben saying to the other officer? His eyes had been as big as coffee saucers when we arrived and probably still were. Where did that piece of crack rock we purchased for 600 bucks go?

An endless stream of questions flooded my mind as the police officer returned to my window and instructed me to exit the vehicle, "Let's cut the shit. We know you and your buddy came here to buy drugs. So if you confess now, we'll go easy on you." He raised his eyebrows questioningly. "We can do this the easy way or the hard way—the choice is yours," he added. My thoughts were clouded, and I struggled to think logically then; lying seemed the easiest option. If we were going to get caught with crack, it would be the same whether it was a gram or an ounce, so I just said, "Sir, I don't do drugs. I made a wrong turn and ended up in this war zone, and I am trying to get out of here and go home." He smiled slightly and replied, "Okay then, looks like it's the hard way." "What in the hell did he mean by the hard way?" I thought. The officer's choice of words sent a chill down my spine!

The officer commanded me to put my hands in the air. At that moment, I was sure I had screwed myself past the point of no return. He informed me he would handcuff me for our mutual safety. How kind of him. I asked if I was under arrest, and he replied with an arrogant smirk as if to say, 'Not yet.' He secured the handcuffs and walked me back to the police car, where Ben waited in the back seat. Before I could sit down, Ben winked at me and whispered, "I already told them we got lost." Without further discussion, we watched a huge German Shepherd emerge from another patrol car, wagging its tail profusely. The thought, "We're screwed, we're screwed, we're screwed again," raced through my mind as the mammoth canine passed us by. It seemed to sneer at me as if it were saying, "Gotcha motherfucker!"

Officer Cujo jumped into the car's back seat as if a delicious steak was waiting for him to devour. Little did we know it would be our asses on the line once the cops discovered the golf ball made of crack. I felt my reality crash as Ben and I waited in the patrol car while Super Dog searched our car. My heart dropped when I saw the German Shepherd walk away. Had they not found it? Did Ben eat it in such a short period? The golf ball hadn't magically vanished. Did Ben have some David Copperfield shit up his sleeve?

It blew my mind when the officer opened the back door and said, "Okay, both of you get out." He continued and offered us a deal: if we gave him the drugs, he'd go easy on us. We thought the same thing simultaneously—the cops hadn't found them yet. Ben spoke up, and I thought, oh no, shut up! All I wanted to do was go home. The officer wasn't buying it; he told the other cop to pat us down— HARD. But what did HARD mean? I soon found out: they rubbed every single part of my body, even lifting my nut sack through my shorts and making me bend over while spreading my cheeks apart. They did the same to Ben, but still nothing, no drugs.

I politely inquired, "May we go home now, sir?" assuring him I wouldn't make the same mistake again and he'd never see our car in this area. I was subconsciously thinking about which body orifice they would check next, and this made my insides laugh and relax.

He agreed, and they took off the handcuffs. We calmly returned to the car as three police cars started their vehicles one at a time and slowly drove away as if in a funeral procession.

I watched as the supporting cast of the Thriller music video reappeared in the streets, and the scene returned to its normal state. I smirked. The 24-hour thriller video was beginning again, and all was right with the world.

We drove in silence so I could concentrate on the road without distraction. We pulled up at my apartment complex after an eternity, but it was only around 15 minutes. "What just happened?" I asked. "We were fortunate," Ben replied. Anger welled up inside of me as I demanded to know why he'd taken us down into a war zone. His answer didn't satisfy me; he said he had been that way many times before, and nothing had happened. We walked into my apartment, sitting on the couch across from the window, which overlooked the parking lot. Ben stood up and opened the blinds, looking out at his car for 30 minutes, almost like he thought someone would break in or get it towed away. I couldn't take it anymore and asked if he thought they were following us home. Ben said no, but my crack-smoking friend was checking to ensure they had kept us from trailing here. I told him it would be best if he left tomorrow. I had no hard feelings, but this situation wasn't working out.

"That's cool," Ben said in response. "Hey man, can I get my keys?" Ben asked. "Sure, here you go," I said as I tossed him the keys from across the couch. "Walk out to the car with me; I want to show you something," he continued. Immediately, my mind began racing, wondering what kind of trick he had now. Ben opened the driver's door and told me to enter the passenger seat. "I'm not going anywhere right now, bro," I replied. "Me neither," he casually responded. "Check this out," he said as I watched in awe while he worked his magic. He started the engine, put his foot on the brake pedal, put the car into reverse, and then back into the park again - though we weren't going anywhere. After completing this sequence and turning the key off, the stereo slid before us, revealing a small box containing the golf ball-sized crack we bought half an hour ago. "Are you fuckin' kidding me?" I asked, in shock at what he had revealed to me. "Trap door, my brother," he said triumphantly.

"C'mon, let's head back to your place, and I'll explain it all." He grabbed the crack rock and put it in his shirt pocket; then, we walked back to my apartment. "What on earth happened in the car?" I asked as he plopped the golf-ball-sized lump of crack down onto the glass table. "Yeah, I know what happened was insane, but just let's take one hit, and I'll be off," he said. My opiate-addled brain thought it would be alright to have just one hit.

Ben stepped into the kitchen and grabbed the 2-liter, single-person rocket ship from its launching pad on the table before us. I watched in awe as he took out a 14-gram rock that looked like an actual golf ball, and he expertly cut two pieces off it with a razor blade. The larger piece went on top of the ashes in the makeshift bowl atop the two-liter bottle. "You get to go first this time," he said. As I recall, I almost refused—this was my second chance to say no. In hindsight, no is probably the best word in the dictionary; two little syllables could have transformed my life. But as it is, saying yes fits into God's more excellent plan for me: teaching me a valuable lesson in life and putting me where I am today—with a beautiful wife, angelic dog, and loving family. So, instead of refusing, I bent over and put the pen stem of the bottle into my mouth, lit it with a lighter, and watched as the crack dissolved slowly into the ashes.

I gasped out my last breath as he said, "Pull easy." As I followed his orders, a thick smoke filled the two-liter bottle. The smoke seemed more concentrated this time around. "Let go of the carburetor," he ordered. As soon as I did, the dense smoke vanished completely—first into my lungs and then directly to the dopamine center in my brain. It's hard to explain if you've never smoked crack, but the immediate feeling of intense euphoria is so powerful it takes your breath away. Remember how you felt as a kid when you first discovered masturbation and experienced that orgasmic euphoria for the very first time? That's what it was like, only it lasted for about five minutes! After each hit of the demon's dust, I could only say wow.

That incident eventually lasted an entire week, and now that I'm sixty years old, with twenty-four years having passed since then, all I remember is a blur. On my right thumb, there's still a callus from flicking the Bic lighter hundreds of times over that period. To this day, it serves as a daily reminder - not a fond one, but one that makes me feel sick to my stomach. It's an experience I wish I could erase forever. It was only by sheer luck I found my way out of the mess. Eventually, after spending ten thousand dollars, I kicked Ben out. His erratic behavior - day or night, light or dark - demanding the vertical blinds be closed out on the patio didn't help. Left alone, I would have spent all the sixty-six thousand dollars from my settlement.

I lived on the first floor, and Ben insisted cops watch over us in the parking lot. Ben's paranoia was not very pleasant to witness, so I had warned him that if he uttered another word regarding police presence in the lot, he would need to leave. After taking another big hit, Ben sat on the sofa and commented that he thought undercover officers were hanging around my parking lot. I said nothing but forcefully got up off the couch and briskly marched over to the vertical blinds. I yanked them open with such force that some broke free from their fixtures. Then I flung the sliding glass doors open and yelled, "Here we are! If you're out there, put us out of our misery!" Ben just stared at me, wide-eyed with fear. I commanded Ben to grab his shit and get out, and he got the hell out of my apartment. After I defeated the Devil, I was exhausted and done dealing with him. Before closing the door behind him, I uttered a last goodbye: "Take care, bro."

" Hell is empty and all the devils are here."

William Shakespear

Chapter 17

Who Can It Be Now

"Wow! What a week," I somberly thought after Ben left my apartment. Looking back, it probably cost me a quarter of my brain cells plus ten thousand dollars. What a nightmare. But now he was gone, and I could get back to my poor, pathetic life of chasing pills. By this time in my addiction, the usual dose I was taking was ten of the 10 milligrams of Lortab, usually 3, sometimes four times a day. Since 10 was such a mouthful, I just started putting them in a coffee cup with a bit of water and dissolving them, then drinking them. My stomach began to moan and groan, and then I honestly thought back and couldn't remember when I had last eaten. I dialed up my go-to Chinese and awaited General Tao's arrival.

After half an hour later, General Tso showed up with the grub. I'd tasted nothing quite like it before! Every bite and each one seemed to have even more flavor than the last. It was as if there was a party going on in my mouth. I had been without food for so many days that everything tasted much better! By the time I finished, I had not left a grain of rice in the red and white Chinese boxes. I drifted off to sleep around 8 PM, having promised myself I'd call my friend first thing in the morning to get more pills because I knew tomorrow would be unbearable without them. As I dozed off, my usual dream started playing out: an airplane crash that somehow miraculously had me living but walking through body parts and coffins in what appeared to be a hangar. Why did this harrowing nightmare haunt me night after night? Even my nightmares paled compared to the ugly reality that was unfolding before me. My thoughts wandered down a dark tunnel. I had never encountered this kind of despair before. It wasn't quite suicidal, but it was teetering dangerously close. I wanted to run away from the pain and yet felt strangely compelled to stay. All of it made me question my sanity as well as my mortality.

Would my life end in one of the most extreme ways imaginable, with them picking up my incinerated body parts and putting them in a bag for burial? Or would I live a long, prosperous life before finally succumbing to old age? As unlikely as it may be, I was still more inclined to bet on the former; there was no way I was going to die of a natural death at my age! At this rate, I barely expected to make it past 38. My entire life had become about simply making it through each day. At about 5 o'clock, I took the last 10 Lortabs I had. Seeing that empty baggie that now only contained a bit of light bluish dust was a sad, sad thought. The little monster began rambling in my brain, " You better find more pills. You know what happens if you don't feed me? I will kick your ass and give you the darkest thoughts you have ever had. I finally fell asleep about 8 o'clock, promising myself and the lil monster to call my buddy as soon as I awoke.

I didn't wake up until noon the next day. I had slept 16 hours, which was not surprising considering I had barely gotten an hour or two of sleep the entire week. When I finally rose, I felt stuck to the sheets and smelled terrible, a mix of rotten fruit and a wet dog.

Sitting up made me feel as if I were riding a carnival ride with no brakes, and I could barely contain the bile surging up my throat. The little monster inside me started screaming at me to find more pills or suffer dire consequences—I knew all too well what would come if I didn't listen. Reaching for my nightstand, I dialed my friend's number on the phone, but it rang for what seemed like an eternity of ringing before I gave up and hung up the phone. The little monster would not be happy.

The lil monster kept asking me, "What are you going to do?" repeatedly. I had no answer, and the hopelessness threatened to overwhelm me. I slowly made my way to the bathroom and started brushing my teeth. Instead of enjoying it like usual, it felt more like a wire brush against my gums. Every time I touched, excruciating pain shot through my head. What is wrong with me? Right then, an ultra-vibrant yellow acidic vomit spewed out of my throat and sprayed around the two-foot radius of the sink. It was almost like radioactive waste from a nuclear reactor, only this stuff was coming from my stomach. I hurriedly rinsed out the bathroom sink, trying not to see the substance ever again while my stomach began cramping fiercely. This wasn't normal constipation; it was something different that urged me to rush onto the toilet.

The entire time I was vomiting and having diarrhea, the little monster in my head was roaring at me. I felt like death incarnate! I had to find something to make me feel better. This expelling of bodily fluids was by far the worst experience of my life, and I wished there were ten Lortabs dissolved in a cup of water so I could take them, but there weren't. My mind wandered through an unfamiliarly negative space, someplace it had never been before, though not quite suicidal, but only a notch below.

I lay back down again, wondering what to do: go to another hospital's ER or wait and see. As I mulled over my options, I collapsed into a deep sleep, almost like one gets before an operation. It was so deep that Flight 666, which I usually rode in my dreams, flew past without me getting burned up this time.

A heavy knock rapped against the door leading from my primary bedroom to the patio. I thought I heard Ben's voice, and my heart sank. He was back. I stayed still, hoping he'd disappear if I made no sound. Three more knocks echoed through the room, each louder than the last. "Jimmy, I know you're in there," a voice boomed from the other side of the thin door between us. "I'm not leaving until you open the door, so you might as well just do it," the voice continued, but it sounded more feminine this time. Who in the hell was this? I had no girlfriend, and I was pretty damn sure it wasn't my wife. I'm sure she was hoping I would stay in my lil hell hole and only speak to her again when it involved something with the children. Then it hit me.

The voice was familiar; I knew it was Dina. Dina was the wife of my buddy, Ryan, who had recently gone to prison for a three-year sentence. Dina was not one to give up quickly, so with a sense of dread, I said, "Just a minute," and scrambled to find some clothes. As soon as I opened the door and stepped out into the sunshine, I felt like its blazing heat had melted through me.

"You look like crap," Dina commented as she walked into the room. I had met her a few years back when Ryan and I opened a Cajun restaurant in Florida. They began dating and eventually got married. After we moved back to Lexington, Ryan ran into some trouble; he had been on probation before, so they put him in jail this time. Despite this, Dina decided to still move up to Kentucky with him. Ultimately, the situation didn't go well for either of them. "My god, you look like you've been hit by a train!" she said, shaking her head. "Thanks.. nice to see you too," I replied weakly. "Jimmy, what have you been doing? You look horrible," she asked. I answered with an exhausted shrug: "You don't want to know." Dina sighed and continued: "Get up and shower. I'm going to get you out of this apartment today."

The small voice in my head was screaming, telling me I had to get pills or else everything would be like a horror movie today. I knew it was right, so I had no choice. My friend told me to take a shower while she waited. "What is that smell?" she asked. I had hidden in this crack den for the past week and couldn't tell. "It smells like something died in here, and you burned and buried it," she exclaimed. "I guess I forgot to take out the garbage," I said nonchalantly. "That's the strangest garbage smell I've ever smelled," she continued. "Like a cross between sewage and some kind of burning chemical." "Alright," I sighed, "I'll spray some Febreeze or Lysol." She nodded and said, "Get a shower and let's go."

The lil monster piped up with his usual demand: "What are you going to do, what are you going to do, what are you going to do?" He threatened he would make me feel awful if I didn't get some pills right away. My head was spinning from the week of crack cocaine indulgence, and this time, I had no answer for him. It rooted him in the depths of my brain, in the dark and dismal parts that only he lived in, the part that produced all of my evil thoughts. My inner voice struggled to reply, "I don't know!" Worrying scenarios raced through my mind as I searched desperately for a solution that did not involve getting pills. Dina stared at me like I was a three-headed sea creature she'd found on the beach.

"I'm exhausted from the week. I need some sleep," I said harshly this time. "Just a few more hours should do it," I continued, and Dina felt my change in tone. "Okay," she conceded, "but you could use a home-cooked meal." I laughed inwardly, knowing I had only eaten a Chinese meal the prior week. Ben and I had eaten nothing else.

I must sleep a few more hours before I can do anything." I reiterated firmly. "Sounds fair?" Her expression softened. "Yes, come to my place at seven, and I'll make our Italian food. Please bring some red wine!" she instructed. "I'll be there on time!" I responded, ushering her out of the door. Behind it, I peeked through the blinds and watched her drive away before finally letting out a sigh of relief as my little monster started up his usual song and dance.

" You can get the monkey off your back, but the circus never leaves town."

Anne Lamott

Chapter 18

"Chasing the Dragon"

The instant Dina stepped out of my apartment, my mind started racing. I sank back into my bed, knowing that I wouldn't be able to go anywhere without getting some pills first. What can I do? It was a recurring thought that kept running through my head. There were still two weeks left until Rick could give me the pills I needed. Was I going to resort to a four-hour emergency room visit? Would they be able to tell that I was lying, or would they find massive amounts of crack cocaine in my system and forcibly admit me to a psych ward until I was clean? My thoughts were whirling like an EF-5 tornado.

I rushed back and forth to the bathroom, trying to get rid of any remaining fluids. Even with all the pain I had experienced in my life - football injuries, car crashes - this was by far the worst. In every other negative situation, I had always looked for the positive, but this time, it seemed impossible. This was different. I felt completely and utterly helpless. Everywhere I looked, there was no glimmer of hope, nothing to hang on to in my darkest hour. There was a void inside me. The little haven of positive thought I always turned to for strength had disappeared. I wanted to scream out and yell, "Fuck it, I can beat this!" but with every breath I took, the emptiness within me only grew.

Fear and despair consumed me. It felt like I had descended into a vast, dark abyss with no way out. My mind ventured to places it had never been, and I wouldn't say I liked it. This was completely unfamiliar territory for my 36-year-old self. All I wanted was to return to being my old self, who saw the glass as half full. This place scared me; it terrified me! I never knew this dreadful chasm existed within my mind, and now that I had opened it up, I wanted nothing more than to close it off forever. Still in the dark of my apartment, my head filled with these crippling thoughts; I had just about called Ben and see if he had any pills when the phone rang. "Hey man, do you need anything?" came the familiar gravelly voice. "Yes, sir," I answered with an unexpected energy. "I got a hundred for you if you want them," Ben said. Of course I want them, I thought to myself; there was nothing else I desired more right now. "Of course I want them. When can I come to pick them up?" I replied. "I have to go out for a while, but I will be back around seven," Ben informed me.

My mind raced, thinking of everything I had to do. I had promised Dina I would be over at 7 o'clock for dinner, and it was already 3 in the afternoon. The little monster inside me was saying fuck her. "What's more important, her or pills? " Ben asked. This was a no-brainer, I thought. I desperately needed to get pills and get well!

Can't I just run over and get them now?" I asked calmly." I have to leave now; you better wait until seven when I get back," he said, but the little monster shouted angrily inside my head, "Fuck him! Just get them now, or you'll be miserable for four hours!" My brain rapidly searched for a good reason. I couldn't wait until 7. It also occurred to me that he could make an extra hundred dollars from this deal, so he wanted me to get them from him. Drawing on my poker-playing skills, I bluffed out of this situation. "I'm sorry, but I have to leave town around five o'clock and won't be back till the end of the week," I said solemnly.

After an unbearable wait, he finally replied to my bluff with the words I longed to hear. "Can you come over right now?" It overwhelmed my mind with relief and happiness when I heard those sweet words. The lil monster in my head screamed," Fucking A, we can come get them now!" "I can be there in 15 minutes!" I responded with excitement. Before hanging up, I could hear him urging me to hurry. It's wild how addiction works! After suffering from withdrawals - retching, shitting continuously, and sweating profusely for days on end, knowing that pills were coming soon would make me feel better instantly. This addiction is both psychological and physical, and I'm not ashamed to admit that it can take you closer to insanity than you've ever been.

Your body will start rejecting every fluid you have inside of you, making you feel like death warmed over. But once you realize the pills are going to arrive within an hour, something unusual happens inside your head; at least it did to me. The depressing thoughts that circled in my head vanished as if by magic. Despite not having anything introduced into my bloodstream, I no longer experienced physical pain or discomfort.

As I left the building, a small smile showed that my mind was much more regular and happy than it had been for the last few hours. I often wonder if they just gave me a placebo for the medicine

I took. It is bizarre to see how these opioids can change one's mental state. As I walked out to my car, everything felt brighter, and I even had an extra bounce.

A mere second later, however, the negative thoughts would return and darken my mental landscape unless I could get back to feeling great, with the reassuring thought that "everything will be alright" circling in my head again. On my way to achieving this utopia, traffic congested as I got closer and closer, and those unpleasant thoughts started returning. The joyous ride my mind went on when finding out I could get some pills quickly dissipated.

"Run the light!" the little monster screamed. As I spoke with the mischievous character, my car took off when the light turned green. The next few lights played out similarly, and I got closer to his apartment with each passing second. A feeling of anticipation for what was to come filled me like a warm blanket on a winter evening. I started laughing, thinking that there should be a particular lane on the highway for people going to get dope. As I pulled into the lot of Ben's apartment, I couldn't help but laugh. When Ben opened the door, he asked me why it took so long. "A lot of red lights," I replied. He chuckled and said he thought I must've sprouted wings and flown over all the traffic since I'd arrived so quickly. I thought sarcastically in my mind, 'Ha ha ha,'

"Motherfucker, just give me the pills and shut tha fuck up," the lil monster yelled at the top of his voice. "Here you go, bro," Ben said as he handed me a plastic bag filled with the blue football-shaped pills I depended on. "Cool," I replied, giving him the freshly minted $100 bills I had taken from my closet before coming over there. My addiction was so strong that now I keep six of these bills in my closet at all times so I wouldn't have to waste time going to an ATM for more money when getting my pills. After picking up my pills and heading back home, I'd always stop by the ATM for another six $100 bills and replace the ones in my closet. "I'm out, thanks, brother," I said. "Oh, can I use your bathroom real quick?" "Sure, it's the first door on the right down the hall," he answered. As usual, as soon as I started walking out the door, the little monster inside me kept screaming until I did what it wanted. So, before leaving his house, I went into the bathroom and took ten pills.

Throughout the fifteen years that I fought my opioid addiction, my mind kept feeding me the same lie every time I was about to get pills or just after scoring them. "You can quit when these run out - you can wean yourself off and just stop." It's odd: I believed it every time. If I had to estimate, I'd say I bought pills 500-600 times. Anyway, here I was in Ben's bathroom; ten pristine 10mg blue Lortab tablets stood before me. Swallowing a handful of pills had become second nature to me; practice makes perfect, right?

His video game still distracted Ben, and I waved as I left his house. I drove to the ATM to get cash, then went home without trouble. The hydrocodone took effect, but its initial warmth blanket of comfort felt diminished from before. It still reassured me with the feeling that "everything will be alright," but it didn't provide the same exhilarating sensation as when I first took those Percocet pills and experienced a euphoric high. All people with an opiate addiction know it's like chasing a dragon, always trying to replicate that sensation of your very first experience with opioids.

We who have been addicted to opioids know that the high never matches the first time, but we continue to chase it around the same vicious circle. It's like riding a merry-go-round at top speed, and you can't get off! The euphoric rush might not be the same, but it still gets you just as high, and that's where addiction lies. When you don't have them in your system, the brutal sickness and withdrawals become the main reason you continue to stay addicted. It's an experience like no other: physical sickness combined with mental exhaustion. Withdrawal takes you to a place in your brain that, if you're lucky, you'll never want to visit or go back to. A deep, dark corner filled with despair and hopelessness. The one place I had kept myself away from my whole life until now. It's a cavernous abyss telling me life is not worth living anymore.

I returned to my apartment with the lingering scent of crack weaving its way around me. A glance at the clock on my nightstand showed it was almost five thirty, and I had an hour and a half before I was supposed to head over to Dina's for dinner. Damn, I muttered under my breath; why did I agree to this? After constant questioning about Ryan being sent away to Lexington, Kentucky's Blackburn Federal Prison, for three years, I knew what she'd be. How could I get out of this? I considered every excuse imaginable, but nothing seemed to satisfy Dina. Ultimately, I resigned myself to going once and getting it over with. For the next hour, I lay there until six thirty, then got up and gulped down ten more Lortabs before heading out the door towards Dina's house for a night of awkward small talk.

" It is not necessary to change. Survival is not mandatory."

W. Edwards Deming

Chapter 19

Dinner and a Convict

☐   "Hey there, what's going on?" Dina opened the door to her

apartment and asked me. "Not much," I replied. "Good news is you

look much better than you did five hours ago," Dina said jokingly

yet seriously. "Yeah, I feel much better, too," I laughed. "What have

you been doing all week?" she asked earnestly. "Not much. Why

haven't you called me back? I left you several messages last week,"

she said. Dina spoke in a sad monotone, "I needed to talk to you about Ryan. He's been challenging; since he's been in jail, I've given him everything he asks for, but every time I visit, Ryan complains about everything." "I'm sure it must be hard for him mentally, knowing that he has to stay behind bars for three years, but taking his frustration out on his wife isn't the way to go," I commented. "He even said he wanted to get a divorce the last time I saw him," she said while tears fell from her eyes.

Ryan has been my closest friend for over fifty years. We used to spend our weekends together at the country club, playing golf and swimming. He is one of those friends who would jump in a fight with you or defend you instantly. He's also known for having strict standards. So when I asked him if he truly loved the girl he was about to marry, his response clarified that he wasn't head-over-heels: "Well, everyone gets married eventually, right? Might as well marry her; she's probably just as good as anyone else." That sealed it for me—I knew his marriage wouldn't last. It didn't last.

"He's struggling right now, Dina," I replied calmly. "Next time you talk to him, tell him he can call me, and I'll lend an ear." "Thanks, I don't know what else to do," she said. "How have things been with you?" "Just tryin' to get by," was all I could muster. I couldn't tell her the truth that I was taking 30-40 10mg Lortab pills a day and that I had just gone through a week of smoking around a pound of crack cocaine. Or about this little monster in my head that demanded I never go without opioids running through my veins ever again? Every time I ran out, I became damn near suicidal; no, it would be best to keep all those thoughts in my head. It was scary enough there! I shuddered to think how any rational person would react if they heard what was happening inside my head. They would lock me up in a padded cell.

I knew I had to confront the beast I'd created, and it would be a fight to the death—. Little did I know this battle would take fifteen long years. How I survived it all and write about it now is a miracle. That's why I'm saying that if I could make it through, you can too. All you need is the willpower and desire to quit and get your life back. It's that simple. Well, simple might not be the correct term. It will be your most complex challenge, but when the dust clears, you will have a life. And I will show you how I did it and help you do the same.

So, where were we? Ah, yes. I ate a big dinner at Dina's and listened to her go on for hours about her complicated relationship with Ryan like any good friend would do when they needed someone to lean on. When I couldn't take it anymore, I said I'm exhausted, Dina. That home-cooked meal was just what I needed." She wished me well as I left through the door.

Throughout the following few weeks, everything was fine. I even received a collect call from Ryan in jail, where he told me something that I could never tell Dina. Ryan said he didn't love her and wanted her out of his apartment and Kentucky. I humbly listened and told him to consider his decisions while serving his three-year prison sentence. He said he had thought it through and preferred being alone forever. He ended up divorcing Dina and is still single to this day, twenty-three years later.

"The presence of fear and darkness does not mean that the hopeful parts of me cease to exist."

Erin Frye

Chapter 20

Keep On Rollin' Baby

☐   "Hey there, what's going on?" Dina opened the door to her apartment and asked me. "Not much," I replied. "Good news is you look much better than you did five hours ago," Dina said jokingly yet seriously. "Yeah, I feel much better, too," I laughed. "What have you been doing all week?" she asked earnestly. "Not much. Why haven't you called me back? I left you several messages last week," she said. Dina spoke in a sad monotone, "I needed to talk to you about Ryan. He's been challenging; since he's been in jail, I've given him everything he asks for, but every time I visit, Ryan complains about everything." "I'm sure it must be hard for him mentally, knowing that he has to stay behind bars for three years, but taking his frustration out on his wife isn't the way to go," I commented. "He even said he wanted to get a divorce the last time I saw him," she said while tears fell from her eyes.

Ryan has been my closest friend for over fifty years. We used to spend our weekends together at the country club, playing golf and swimming. He is one of those friends who would jump in a fight with you or defend you instantly. He's also known for having strict standards. So when I asked him if he truly loved the girl he was about to marry, his response clarified that he wasn't head-over-heels: "Well, everyone gets married eventually, right? Might as well marry her; she's probably just as good as anyone else." That sealed it for me—I knew his marriage wouldn't last. It didn't last.

"He's struggling right now, Dina," I replied calmly. "Next time you talk to him, tell him he can call me, and I'll lend an ear." "Thanks, I don't know what else to do," she said. "How have things been with you?" "Just tryin' to get by," was all I could muster. I couldn't tell her the truth that I was taking 30-40 10mg Lortab pills a day and that I had just gone through a week of smoking around a pound of crack cocaine. Or about this little monster in my head that demanded I never go without opioids running through my veins ever again? Every time I ran out, I became damn near suicidal; no, it would be best to keep all those thoughts in my head. It was scary enough there! I shuddered to think how any rational person would react if they heard what was happening inside my head. They would lock me up in a padded cell.

I knew I had to confront the beast I'd created, and it would be a fight to the death—. Little did I know this battle would take fifteen long years. How I survived it all and write about it now is a miracle. That's why I'm saying that if I could make it through, you can too. All you need is the willpower and desire to quit and get your life back. It's that simple. Well, simple might not be the correct term. It will be your most complex challenge, but when the dust clears, you will have a life. And I will show you how I did it and help you do the same.

So, where were we? Ah, yes. I ate a big dinner at Dina's and listened to her go on for hours about her complicated relationship with Ryan like any good friend would do when they needed someone to lean on. When I couldn't take it anymore, I said I'm exhausted, Dina. That home-cooked meal was just what I needed." She wished me well as I left through the door.

Throughout the following few weeks, everything was fine. I even received a collect call from Ryan in jail, where he told me something that I could never tell Dina. Ryan said he didn't love her and wanted her out of his apartment and Kentucky. I humbly listened and told him to consider his decisions while serving his three-year prison sentence. He said he had thought it through and preferred being alone forever. He ended up divorcing Dina and is still single to this day, twenty-three years later.

"Life is like a carousel; You aim for heaven and you wind up in hell."

Bad Company

Chapter 21

Better Ingredients, Better Pizza; Fast, Free, Unfriendly Delivery

I moved all my stuff on Saturday, and Daryl took over my old

apartment. The next few weeks are foggy, but I remember telling

Dina I'd start splitting bills as soon as I found a job. She would talk endlessly about how Ryan was treating her, but I knew his actual intentions did not match up with what she thought. I needed to get employed quickly for money and to save myself from all the crying about Ryan. So, I started scanning the classifieds in search of an ideal job with afternoon and night shifts available.

I stumbled into the perfect position for me that ticked all my boxes. A 5 pm-1 am shift. Plenty of cash flowing in and out. It seemed like destiny, and my resume matched every qualification they sought. That, paired with the fact that I always got hired, fueled my confidence that I would get this job, too. It wasn't false confidence, either. I applied for the job, went through an interview process, and got hired.

In my mornings, I was used to being tortured, filled with depressing thoughts and constant screaming from the little monster. I would wake up an hour before getting up, feeling like a bus had run over me. Dry heaving and having the most depressing thoughts! I would then take the ten pills I had laid on the nightstand the night before and lay back down, waiting to be whisked away to Neverland.

Waking up just brought out the most depressing, debilitating thoughts any human mind could have. Between these thoughts and the lil monster screaming his head off to be fed, mornings weren't my favorite time of day.

Even several decades later, I'm still plagued by those same feelings when I wake up. The brain is a remarkable organ - easily trained but never forgetting its traumas. Despite being 60 years old now and beginning to lose my memory, it's kept that fifteen-year block of hell alive in my head. Of course, I hope not to have dementia or Alzheimer's in my later years; however, if I did, at least that part would be gone. It sure would be nice for my brain to forget certain things! And 25 years on, I still don't enjoy mornings.

After my training was complete, I started my shifts as planned. The first few weeks went smoothly—I was having my pills delivered while I worked and then returning home around 1:30 in the morning. I'd usually eat some leftover pizza and go straight to bed around 3 am. This pattern continued every single day.

Dina was a bank teller. I know how ironic. My roommate was a bank teller, and I had a drug problem. Thankfully, I did nothing stupid, like trying to rob her bank or doing anything too stupid. Maybe further in my addiction, I might have. It was a straightforward arrangement. Dina worked 9-5, so we hardly ever saw each other unless I was fortunate enough to have a weekend day off. That was perfect because I needed and wanted to be left alone in my lil cloud of drug haziness. Why bring anyone else into this nightmare I was living daily?

The following month went on without incident. I had gotten myself in a position where I owed about $1,000 to some dealers, and they were starting not to want to bring me any pills until I paid them back. I needed to find a new dealer where I could start at 0.

Fortunately, as I was pondering this, my friend Ben called me and asked if I had ever taken any pills by the name of OxyContin. Not having tried them before, I replied no. He then told me that his buddy had gotten his hands on some and wondered if anyone wanted to try it out. It was 1999, and these kinds of drugs were becoming available on the streets, so people were all for trying it out. I agreed to give it a go, providing he gave me a sample since I didn't want to waste my finances on something I hadn't tried before. He laughed at my request and offered to provide Junior with - yes, his name was Junior - my number. That night, I went off to work with ten tabs running through my veins and another 10 I set aside for my dinner break time. My cell phone rang, showing an unknown number. I answered and heard, "Hello Jimmy, this is Junior, a friend of Ben. Would you be interested in sampling some 'Florida Oranges' that are being shipped up from Florida?" he asked.

Ben had said the guy was cool but paranoid, so I affirmed his claims and chuckled. I offered him a sizeable extra pepperoni pizza if he brought me a few oranges. "Sounds good, man," I replied. Those three brief words began my journey with OxyContin. It became known as "Hillbilly Heroin." Purdue Pharma makes this pure narcotic in an environmentally controlled lab—unlike Colombian jungle drugs that are cut with substances from baby laxatives to gasoline. Oxys were pure, uncut oxycodone. The strongest and best pain medication ever produced. Ask anyone who has ever traveled down the opioid highway, and they will all tell you,

" It just doesn't get any better than Oxys. They are at the top of the opioid food chain, trust me!

At 6:58 pm, one of my workers peered into my office and shouted, "Jimmy! There's someone at the front counter asking for you!" My inner excitement soared, and the little monster inside me jumped up and down joyfully. When I arrived at the front counter, I extended my hand to meet Junior's and said, "Hey, I'm Jimmy. Nice to meet you". He returned the brotherly handshake and handed me a mesh bag full of oranges that seemed to come straight from Florida. After he received his pizza, I said I'd be in contact before long, and I will never forget his response; he looked me straight in the eyes with no hesitation and said, "Yes, you will." We said our goodbyes. And I returned to my tiny office, where I locked the door.

Thanks to the tinted windows, I had a clear view outside while remaining hidden from others. I took out an orange bag and carefully checked the contents. Each orange contained a green pill in its navel, which someone had carved and covered with a coating of bright orange marker. The dealer must have been paranoid. Junior told me the pills were time-released, so all I needed to do was wash away the coating, crush them up, and snort them. So that's what I did: I put the pill in my mouth and rolled it around my tongue for a minute or two until I could feel the roughness of the underlying pill on my tongue, and all the time-release coating had melted away. I crushed it with a lighter under a dollar bill and rubbed it with a credit card until there were no pieces bigger than dust. This was a technique I'd learned from using another drug before.

Without hesitation, I bent down, picked up a dollar bill, and did exactly what you would expect me to do. I carefully scraped the OxyContin residue stuck to the money into a line, which would be the first of many during my fifteen-year "run." It would be at least one thousand lines if I had to guess how much I snorted over that period. You could make an incredibly thick line from an 80 mg pill, while a 160 mg pill had enough to create what we called an "8-ball" line - but I'll explain more about that later. After placing the powder in a single line with my makeshift straw, I inhaled it quickly and all at once through one nostril. To ensure I left no residue behind, I went to the restroom to use water to clear out my nasal passage before returning to my post on the store floor, where several other employees were milling about.

At first, nothing happened—which made me think these Oxys weren't as good as I thought. Then suddenly, BAM! Everything changed. It felt like they had taken me to 3a place in my mind I'd only gone to twice before in my life, during which someone had administered intravenous morphine at the hospital. Waves of warmth engulfed my entire body and mind. This was the best feeling I'd ever experienced in my life! Not even taking Dilaudid straight into my veins could compare. It was like I had reached another level of ecstasy, so much so that if you were to tell me you were going to amputate both of my legs with a chainsaw, I would have said, "No problem, just please clean up the blood!" This ended up being the second-best experience I would ever have within my fifteen-year addiction, but looking back now, it remains one of the most memorable.

The experience was so great that the little monster in my head was speechless — something that had never happened before! All he could get out was "WOW," I hoped it didn't run out. That

shift at work went by like a cool breeze on a clear beach night —
simply stunning. By eleven o'clock, I was still feeling the 80mg Oxy.
I snorted around seven-fifteen, but the little monster insisted I take
the other 80 I had in my pocket. The second blastoff just elevated the
ride that much more. I just sat in my office and almost didn't drive
home. While I was in the place dreams are made of, I wanted
nothing to interrupt my voyage.

I arrived at our apartment around 1:30 am, cautiously
opening the door as quietly as possible. Dina emerged from her room
and said, "Hey, I cooked something tonight, so there are some
leftovers in the fridge for you." I welcomed the news with a laugh
and heated some food before heading to the living room.

Not surprisingly, Dina followed me and began talking about
her Ryan saga again. She spoke calmly yet firmly, saying, "I'm just
going to give him his divorce like he wants and move back to
Florida; I miss my family a lot." My reply was unintentional "Where
the hell am I gonna go?" but it had already popped out of my mouth
before I could think about it. Incredibly, Dina replied with an offer:
"Pack your stuff and come with me. My parents have a big house in

Ocala. My bedroom has been empty since I left". Unsure if her parents would be open to allowing me into their home, I nervously inquired, "Would they be cool with me moving into their house?" To which she responded that they knew of our friendship and would likely welcome helping me in Florida. Considering this proposition, I replied, "Well, yeah, something to think about for sure."

Dina went to bed, and I sat in the lazy boy with many questions running through my very high mind. All I could think about now was getting more oxys, and then all the answers would magically appear. At about 4 am, I could feel the oxy wearing off, and my mind turned into this giant wrecking ball. A big wrecking ball had come alright, and that was me! How in the hell, in a space of 9 months, had I destroyed everything my life had stood for? I couldn't wrap my head around it. This is the night I also realized with an extreme amount of oxycodone running through my mind, sleep was impossible. Who wanted to sleep when you had this witch's brew coursing through your veins?

Oxy provided me with the best high, much better than Lortab or Percocet; it was like a Volkswagen racing a Lamborghini. While hydrocodone was still an option if no Oxys were available, my regular plan was to call the man and get as many Oxys as possible. The little monster inside me that typically stayed put when fed 100 milligrams of hydrocodone now came out and demanded more. He wanted all the Oxys he could get on, yelling, "Call the man and get as many Oxys as you can - NOW!" And, as usual, I followed his orders to a tee.

"What's up, Junior? It's Jimmy?" I asked. "Not much, same old hard work." He replied. "Those oranges you brought last night were superb. Do you have any more to sell?" I inquired in a cheerful voice. "Sure, how many would you like?" Junior answered. In my head, the little monster screamed, "Get em all! Get em all! Get em all!" His greedy aura seemed to radiate off of him. "Can you do 100 for $700?" I questioned gently. "No, but I can do 100 for $800," he stated firmly. "How about $750?" I proposed. Junior happily agreed, and we set a delivery time for four o'clock that day. Just before ending the call, He asked if he could throw in a few pizzas with the order—pepperoni and maybe extra pepperoni. I laughed and said yes. We hung up the phone, and I felt elated.

The initial euphoria subsided as I surveyed my bank balance, which only showed $250 to my name. Darryl still owed me the second half of the deposit, which was 500 bucks. I called him, and he said he would give me the remaining 500 if I could run over now. I set a Guinness record driving over to my old apartment to get the 500 from Darryl because I knew with him that 500 could disappear faster than David Copperfield could see someone in half!

I picked up the cash from Darryl and saw that he had burned a hole the size of a quarter in the new sectional couch I had bought when I first moved in. It was a shame, but I knew what I was getting into with Darryl: he constantly broke stuff without meaning. Despite his carelessness, I loved him like a brother; he was the big brother I had never had.

Darryl would have taken a bullet in the chest for me, and I would have done the same for him. His bullet of choice was a syringe filled with an 8-ball of cocaine. I often wonder what his last thought was after he injected it into his veins. Hopefully, it took effect fast enough that he didn't have time to feel paranoia before succumbing to the drug. Only God knows! My three closest friends all died from overdoses; I can only thank God for my intervention, as it's why I'm here writing this book to save a few lives. Alright, back on track. After withdrawing my last two hundred fifty dollars from the ATM, I headed to work. The 10 Lortabs weren't working like normal, and my mind raced with thoughts of getting those 100 80 mg oxy. That hour between 3 pm - and 4 pm seemed unbearably slow, but then Junior arrived at exactly 4 o'clock and handed me another bag of oranges from Florida. I passed Junior two pepperoni pizzas with $750 tucked inside one box. He opened the pizza box, saw the money rolled up without counting it, and said, "We're good," before driving away.

Someone had shipped a bag of oranges to me, so I quickly entered my office, closed the door, and pulled it out. I laughed out loud at this surprise; he was a genuine character! I poured the oranges onto the ground, but there was nothing else in there - until I saw the bottom of the bag. A cutout piece of cardboard revealed a tightly rolled bundle of 100-80mg oxy! It felt like it flooded my body with either panic or exhilaration - both at once. I remember thinking I would faint from the intensity of it all. After locking up again, I took out the pills and snorted an extensive line of oxy for the third time in my life.

I felt a wave of reassurance wash over me. Then, one of my employees told me a man was here to see me. Turning the corner by the pizza ovens, I saw who it was: one dealer I had owed money to. If he had known I had 100-80mg oxy in my pocket and I had just paid another dealer 750 bucks, it might not have gone as well. He said he'd be back tomorrow, and something terrible would happen if I didn't have his money. All I could say in response was, 'Cool, see ya then.'

He turned and headed for his vehicle, driving by me while motioning as if he were pointing a gun in my direction. An hour later, I received a call with the same demand; "Where's my money?". The walls seemed to inch closer, and I could not stop it. With a sigh, I snorted another oxy and worried about tomorrow. Tomorrow would require $1,000 to set things right, though I needed to find out where it came from. At least the buzz from the oxys erased all the negative shit and replaced them with positive outlooks. Elton reminded me also that the rocket man could always " Burn his fuse up there alone"!

When I got home, Dina was up like usual. She asked if I had thought more about her suggestion of moving to Florida. Time was running out for me to find a new place to live. In my drug-high state, all I could manage was, "Sounds good; when do you think we should move?" She replied that she'd given her notice at work and would leave in five days. When I asked about Ryan's opinion on the matter, she fired back with, "Fuck Ryan! Did he want a divorce? Well, he's going to get one!" I had snorted 3-80s in the last 6 hours, and fuckin catching on fire would have sounded like a good idea to me! In that state of mind, everything sounded good and made sense! I said it sounded like a plan to me and smiled! So, the plan was rolling. Florida, here we come. I needed to dodge a few literal bullets first, though.

" We first make our habits, then our habits make us."

John Dryden

Chapter 22

Remember Dodge Ball?

So there I sat at 3 am, high as hell with 240 mgs of oxy dancing through my mind, body, and soul, and all my brain could muster was, "Don't worry, Jimmy, everything is going to be just fine! I don't remember going to sleep, but apparently, I did and woke up in the lazy boy's chair at about 8 am as Dina was leaving for work. "I'm so excited to move back home, Jimmy. Thanks so much," she said admiringly. "You're welcome. Have a great day, and we can chat later when I get home from work, "I told her. "Ok, she replied, talk to you then." I sat around mostly the rest of the afternoon, snorting oxy and thinking about everyone I owed money to. How was I going to get out of this trap?

I only had two more days at work this week and had told no one of my departure plans! This would be a very covert operation to get out of Lexington without the dealers I owed knowing. I laughed, thinking about the old game of dodgeball you played as a kid in grade school. I would now have to play the best game of dodgeball in my life, and my life, be it living or dying, could be in the balance of my decisions in the next few days. Was crushing up the remaining 80 oxys I had left and snorting them all as quickly as I could just the most simple, obvious answer? It was simple, that's for sure! Probably would be painless, my irrational mind thought. Just slowly transcend into the next realm of life that hopefully was painless, or wholly black and devoid of pain at least! It sounded a lot better than the one I was in now. This one has become a daily nightmare where all I do is to survive the day and get to the next to do the same shit! That's the exact definition of insanity, right?! Doing the same thing over and over, expecting different results, fuck had I already gone insane and just not realized it yet!

Maybe if I crushed up 80-80 mg oxys, made a big infinity circle out of it on my mirrored table, snorted the 64 hundred mg of oxycodone, lay down, went to sleep, and see where I woke up, if at all. Who knows, maybe I would wake up next to Darryl and see the needle that remained in his vein from the eight-ball of coke he had shot and overdosed on. Perhaps he would say, as always.

"What's up, Powers?"' welcome to heaven or hell. I finally snapped out of this detrimental thought pattern. All I had to do was think about what that would have done to my mother. I could do it to myself and everyone else, but not her! I couldn't destroy her life. I could mine, but never hers! This is and was one reason, possibly the only reason I'm writing this and not simply another statistic!

At about 230pm, I crushed up my 3rd oxy of the day and was getting ready for my now famous one snort line, and the little monster chimed in. I was thinking, what tha fuck does this lil demon want? I have fed his greedy ass a steady drip of oxy in the last few days and haven't heard a word from him. This perplexed me greatly!

"Hey man," he said in this rather subtle voice. "Why don't you crush up another one so you don't have to do one as soon as you get to work? One of the first things he had said in a long time that made a bit of sense.". "No, I think this one is fine. " I gently responded. "I wasn't asking you, motherfucker, to crush another pill up. I want to see what two at a time feels like"? That's where he got me. I wondered what snorting 2 - 80s at once would feel like. But of course, he knew; he was living in my head now! Hell, the lil fucker, knew everything, even before I did! I didn't feel like fighting with him and said, "Ok." I casually crushed up another and incorporated it with the first line and lined it all up in 1 big ass line. It made a massive line about 8 inches long and as thick as your pinky finger! One big ass line, I thought before I bent down and again snorted the entire line in one big vacuuming motion. I went through the regular chaotic routine of putting water on my fingertips and snorting to get rid of any powder residue in my nose and to make sure all that shit was getting in my bloodstream and brain. I jumped in my car and was about to drive out of my apt complex, and I'm not going to say BAM! Again, it wasn't a BAM this time as the oxys entered my bloodstream. It was a WOW, WHAT THA FUCK, THIS IS SIMPLY HEAVEN! My euphoric dopamine center had OD'd and entered an utterly mind-blowing space and time It had never been to before. I remember thinking, "OMG, I always want to feel like this. This is nothing short of nirvana, a heavenly-like place right here on Earth in my brain. A party I never wanted to leave. A place where I simply didn't have to worry about a damn thing. My mind, body, and soul had needed a safe place for a very long time, so I wished I could feel this good all the time, or at least that is what my now very high mind was telling me.

I'm trying hard to find an adjective or some way to describe this feeling to you who are reading this and can relate. Most of you reading this or have read it probably know precisely what I'm talking about, but for those who don't, be glad you don't! As a human species, we are not wired to feel this good. That's why it takes the most potent narcotic on planet Earth to get you there. It's the biggest lie the devil has ever told me, and trust me, he has told me many! Remember to kill, steal, and destroy the devil's manifesto to a tee! I now had him taking up residence in my brain, and I did not know how to get him out of it. Well, I learned how but couldn't.

It was that simple. He had me and would not let go quickly! Till death do us part, I thought and laughed, but that was scary as hell, but fuck it, I felt the best I had ever felt in my life! The price I had to pay! I pulled into work, parked, and went in for my 8 hours of making pizza and snorting oxy!

"They say in the end, it's the wink of an eye."

Jackson Browne

Chapter 23

Ready, Set, Let's Get the Hell Out of Here

48 hours. That's all I had left to endure: the phone calls,

threats, and whatever else the dealer might try to do to me. Back in

the day, I always thought drug dealers would be sure to come back

and bring me more pills if I owed them a little something. That is why I always tried to owe all just enough to keep me out of trouble. It's not a very smart way to think, but drugs do that to your brain. Scary, right?

I clocked in, went into my office, and got everything I needed to get done, so my shift ran smoothly. Surprisingly, I was damn good at my job. Imagine how good I would have been not taking pills?! I had put off two dealers I owed money to by telling them I could pay them off in full on Saturday afternoon. Only because I knew I would be halfway through Atlanta by that time. The only dealer I couldn't contact was the one I was most suspicious of. I don't think he would come here and do anything crazy, but who the hell knows? I'm sure he had done much more for much less money than this.

It was about 10:30 pm, and we had been swamped on Thursday night. I had done no oxys since I left home around 3 pm, so my mind was getting in this gray area I didn't like. When that happened, it was never pretty. "Hey motherfucker, I need some oxy dust in my veins!" The little monster had awoken from his slumber and was a bear. The lil' monster demanded not 80 milligrams of oxy but 160 milligrams of the demon dust. "Do two now, and you won't have to do anymore; just do two instead of one now and one at midnight," he rationalized in my now irrational, totally blurred mind. I locked the door in my office and told my workers and drivers I had to make an important phone call and that I wouldn't be available for about 10-15 minutes. I took 2- 80 mg oxys, crushed them up under the dollar bill with the lighter and credit card like I had done a few dozen times before, and what I would do who knows how many damn times in the years to come. I rolled the dollar bill up reasonably tight, bent down, did my now semi-famous inhalation of 160 mg in one continuous line, and slowly raised it. It was like a train rolling full speed down the track, one of those big-ass old-time locomotives with a furnace full of coal, and it hit me head-on. Still, instead of killing me and separating me limb by limb, it shot my mind, soul, and body into space, way out in far outer space, where everything was silent and blissful. Up where I belonged, up where I loved. There were no fears or anguish, just peace and tranquility, or so it seemed. A place I loved to be more than anywhere I had ever been!

I was once more the "Rocketman, burning his fuse up there alone," and I loved it! After the 5-10 minute train ride to space was over, and things leveled off a bit, I opened my office door and walked around. Maybe I should say floated around, to be more precise. I ensured everything was running like a well-oiled machine, and it was! At about midnight, when the drive-through was about to close for the evening, the guy I had working the drive-through came into my office and announced some guy was asking for me at the drive-thru.

"Oh fuck, my mind quickly thought, this can't be good! Just be a regular friend coming by to get a free late-night pizza. It happens now and then, but not much. Considering my luck, probably not tonight! I thought about telling him to tell the guy I wasn't there, but my car was out there, and he knew I was in there. Fuck it, let's face it, I thought, and I walked around the corner. Then, I looked out through the drive-thru opened window. Shit, it was the only person on planet Earth I didn't want to see tonight, and that was the one dealer I couldn't get ahold of. It was also the dealer I owed the most money to.

"I told you I would be back if I didn't get my money, and I'm here! "I tried calling you," I blurted out. "Where's my fucking money, man? This guy was not in the mood for my smooth talk. "I don't have it, but I will Saturday afternoon," my mouth blurted before my brain realized what it had said. It had become my go-to standard bullshit line with all the dealers I owed money to, and he could read through it like a paper-thin card! Before the last syllable came out, a hand clutching a Mac-10 Uzi sideways approached my head in the window from the backseat. All I could see was the hand, and the end of the gun barrel, only an inch from my nose, and the dealer said, "I think I'm going just to have him shoot you now and be done with your white ass." At first, I froze with fear and thought, well, if he does it, it will look like a robbery. If I die, people will think I'm some hero who was stopping my store from being robbed.

When I was snorting oxys, not only would everything be alright, but they made me brave as hell. I felt ten feet tall and bulletproof. This could become incredibly dangerous when you are a guy who isn't scared of much. I just didn't give a fuck, I guess. "Well, you can do that if you choose, and you and your Uzi-carrying brother there in the backseat can go to prison for the rest of your life for over 1000 dollars. I honestly don't give a fuck either way, whether you pull the fuckin' trigger right now or come back Saturday afternoon at exactly 3 pm and get a free extra large pepperoni pizza with ten, one-hundred-dollar bills in the box. We can end our lil arrangement right now. I don't give a fuck, so make a choice. I can die or get back to work. It is up to you!" I couldn't believe I had said this so calmly. We locked eyes after my Dirty Harry-esque Oscar performing speech, and he laughed out loud and said, "You one crazy ass white boy, that's for sure." "Yes, I am," is all I could muster.

"Ok, he said as the faceless hand holding the Uzi retreated to the black hole it had come from. "See you Saturday at 3 pm sharp," he calmly said. "Oh, can you make it two extra large supreme pizzas?" I could not believe my drug-addled ears. "Of course, anything for you, my brother. See you then," and he slowly pulled from the drive-through.

Did that actually happen??? "Oh shit, I hope no one heard or seen anything," I thought to myself. I slowly shut the drive-thru window and locked it to start our closing procedure for the night. To my surprise and delight, everyone was in their little world of doing their closing procedures so they all could get the hell out of there. I walked into my office, locked the door, snorted another 80mg oxy, and started counting money.

After my closing procedures, I turned off all the lights, set the alarm, and locked the front door as if I had not had a Uzi pressed against my face only moments ago. I walked out, sat in my car, and rewound everything that had occurred that night. Yeah, it was time to get the hell out of Kentucky for a while, that was for sure. I had outstayed my welcome, well, at least with all my drug dealers. I walked into the apartment to music blaring and Dina in some maniac state, throwing anything and everything within arm's reach into boxes.

"Hey, what's up?" Dina excitedly said. "Just tired and had a long night at work." Little did she know that she had almost lost her travel companion. "Well, I have everything set up, and I'm going to get the truck after work tomorrow and will start putting what I can into the truck, and when you get home, we can try to finish it up or at least get to a point where we can leave early Saturday morning."

"Sounds like a plan to me, "I said. As I write this, it amazes me and saddens me how easy it was to leave everything I loved. My family, kids, everything my heart truly loved. That's what these damn things do to you, though. They completely take over your mind, soul, and body! They and the devil make you believe that's the most important thing, and after that, "Everything will be just fine!".

I've fought my ass off for the last 15 years trying to put the puzzle of my shattered life back together, and the hard work has paid off. However, some things have changed forever, and regardless of how hard I try, I will never be the same. Life is all about choices. I made mine and have learned to accept that's part of my story. Some things you can't take back, go back, or change. My mother always told me things happen for a reason, and I know they did. I also see that if I hadn't gone through those things, I wouldn't be where I am now, and I love my life now! It took me 25 years to get here, but I love and adore my wife, life, and our little daughter, Lulu, the Brussels Griffon.

I sat and talked with Dina and helped her pack her stuff, and we both went to bed at about 6 am. I worked the next night without incident, and Saturday morning at about 8 am, I loaded the truck with all of our shit, and we both said goodbye to Lexington. Goodbye to our prior lives, as well as Uzi-man! I started the u haul and put it into drive!

" I think hell is somewhere you carry around with you, not where you go."

Neil Gaiman

Chapter 24

Welcome to the Sunshine State, Arrive Alive

We left Lexington at 8 am, as planned. The trip was estimated to be 13-14 hours in the UHaul. I started with 90-80 mg oxy, and by the end of our 15-hour journey, I had snorted nine pills. That's a total of 720 mgs! I took 2 when we left, 2 when we stopped for gas in Knoxville, 2 when we stopped for gas in Atlanta, 2 when we stopped for gas in Valdosta, and one while getting off the ramp in Ocala. We finally arrived at Dina's parents' house at 11 pm. I was so high that I barely said a word, an unusual occurrence for me. My tolerance had grown since I began taking Oxys. When I tried 10 Lortab pills, I barely felt it.

My escape from worry, pain, and regret was becoming increasingly difficult to reach. The door to the special place only I could access had closed slightly. As I lay in my new bed for the first time, my mind raced with questions: was this all a dream? Could I go back to my old life with my wife and kids? No, this was reality, and no matter how much I wished it weren't true, I couldn't change it. I had 81-80 mg of Oxys left; that was enough for me to get through this. I kept repeating those words until finally falling asleep around 3 am.

I had this recurring dream of a plane crash the previous night. Was this a sign of trouble, or was I worrying too much? When Dina asked me what time I would wake up so she could meet her parents, I groggily told her I needed fifteen minutes. That's when an overwhelming feeling of nausea came over me that I had never felt before. I thought I would get sick before she left the room, but luckily, I made it to the bathroom on time. A putrid-smelling, yellow-green bile filled the toilet bowl and tasted sour as it left my mouth. After brushing my teeth as fast as possible and rinsing with minty mouthwash, I grabbed two eighty mg pills from my backpack, crushed them up, snorted them, and got into the shower. After about five minutes, I suddenly felt like a god.

The thing that was so frightening about those little demonic seeds was how quickly they could change your state of mind. You'd feel like you were about to die, then snort a few, and suddenly, you'd be on the other side of the spectrum in minutes – just like flipping a switch! I glanced at myself in the mirror and realized what I saw wasn't all that great, but it was the best I could do now. I entered the kitchen, where Dina's mom and dad were seated around the table. "Welcome to Florida!" her mother exclaimed, echoed by her father. "Thanks, it's nice to be here. Thank you for letting me stay until I'm back on my feet." "No problem," they said together. "We appreciate you taking care of Dina in Kentucky, and you're welcome to stay here as long as you'd like." We all talked for fifteen minutes before Dina's mom had to get to work, luckily right on time.

We were running out of things to talk about, which didn't help the increasing discomfort between us. "What are we up to today?" I asked her. "Well, we're going to have some friends and family over to celebrate my return this evening," she replied. "Sounds great," I said, my enthusiasm failing me. I didn't particularly want to meet a bunch of new people. Although I'd lived in Ocala for about six or seven years previously, I still knew many people who would be coming over. One was an old buddy I had partied with when I lived in Ocala.

The sun warmed my face as I found a chaise lounge by the pool and settled in with my shorts on. They had a nice setup here; with any luck, I could take advantage of it for at least a while - even if I couldn't sustain it indefinitely.

Dina said she would run some errands and reconnect with some old friends. "That's fine; I'll just hang out here by the pool until you return, okay?" I said. As she left the house from the pool entrance, I settled in for some relaxation. But no sooner than I'd got comfortable, the little monster reared his ugly head and proclaimed: 'Hey! Let's snort another eighty.' Damn it - I'd only snorted two of the pills about an hour and a half earlier. Was it possible that they were already losing their effect? Did this mean I would have to start taking ten of them at once as I had with the Lortabs? Even those didn't give me that euphoric buzz anymore; they mostly just kept me from getting sick and managed to keep the voices in my head quiet. Whatever it took to make that happen was worth a moment of peace. So, as usual, I agreed and went into the bathroom. When I returned, Dina's mom asked if I'd like fresh-squeezed lemonade. "Sure, that'd be great!" I said. She told me some were in the refrigerator so that I could help myself whenever. Could life be like this all the time? If it was, then sign me up!

I lay there, feeling the effects of the oxycodone I had snorted. In my head, I heard an endless loop of positive thoughts and encouragement: "Everything is going to turn out alright ."Before I knew it, fifteen minutes had passed, and my skin was getting crisp from being in the Florida sun for too long. I hadn't been exposed to so much sun, and my pale skin showed it. By seven o'clock, when Dina's welcome home pool party started, there were twenty or twenty-five people from family and friends. As I was introduced to many people I didn't know, I felt invincible; the 80s had made me feel like a god. The drugs were dancing around in my brain like ballet dancers—it was perfect!

It was about 10 pm when I heard a truck pull up and someone shout, "Billy's here!" I knew Billy, an old-time friend of mine from Ocala. He saw me and said, "Hey brother, what's happening?" I replied, "Not much. Welcome to Ocala." We Shot tha shit for a few minutes until I asked if he knew anyone who could get me some Pain pills. He seemed surprised by the question and replied, "No, but I got a sack of blow in my truck. Wanna do a line?" Hell yeah, I responded,

Let's do it!

We went out to his truck and snorted a line of Killer

cocaine, talking about topics ranging from its price to the latest in

politics. This blow was terrific; you could tell it hadn't been stepped

on hardly at all. It was light and airy going up your sinuses. This was

the type of cocaine you rarely got a chance to snort. The kind that

didn't burn at all!The type that made you feel great, not paranoid. It

was a great combination with the oxys. I vividly remember that!   I

considered offering Billy an oxy to snort but then thought better of

it. He likely didn't need another substance added to his repertoire.

Especially one that could make him almost suicidal if he ran out.

"We should probably go back inside," I said. "You wanna do one

more line?" he asked. "Hell yeah!" I responded. He split the line into

two even bigger ones this time. We both snorted our lines before

returning to the house and re-entering the pool area where the party

was still going strong. The Little Monster spoke up for the first time

since we had gotten high, saying simply, "Man, oxys and cocaine

work well together; I feel great." I couldn't help but agree with him;

what a buzz! Afterward, I said hi to the crowd before ducking into the bathroom to crush up another oxy onto a dollar bill and snort it in one extensive line.

I had no idea how many oxys I'd snorted that day—it could've been anywhere from six to eight. My mind was clear for the first time in ages, and nothing boggled me; all I knew was that everything would be okay. Midnight rolled around, and the party had begun to die out. I was the last one there with Dina and her parents. She remarked on my pupil size and asked if I could sleep. I assured her I was fine, but Dina offered to help clean up before bed. Jokingly, she suggested that going to bed would be best for me. "Sounds good to me," I mumbled back. With a goodnight, she closed the door and left me to bed.

I won't bore you with a blow-by-blow of every day, but about a week and a half later, I snorted my last oxy at around 6 pm. Usually, I was Snortin' about 6-8 per day - two when I woke up, two at 2 pm, and a couple right before dinner. This kept the little monster locked up in his shit-filled cage, and I'd even begun to think he might have died off. But as soon as I snorted that last oxy, I knew the monster hadn't gone anywhere - he was waiting for me to ask him how I was going to get more pills. It had crossed my mind before, but when I had 50-80mg oxys still in my possession, it wasn't a top priority.

When I woke up the following day after snorting my last oxy, it felt like a wave of panic had swept through me. Withdrawal symptoms set in instantly as soon as my feet touched the floor--even they hurt! Dina and her parents had already left for work, leaving me alone in this unfamiliar place, feeling completely isolated. I felt more depressed than ever before and wondered how I had let myself get into this situation. The little monster in my head kept repeating, 'What the hell are you going to do? I need pills!' For once, I considered ending it all by jumping into the pool at the deep end and staying submerged until my body floated lifelessly to the top. So I lit a cigarette (which wasn't allowed inside the house) and sat outside, wallowing in despair and wanting nothing more than to give up. I was scared to death. I had always had happy tunes running through my head when I was high, but now the song running through my head was " The End" by the Doors." This is the end, beautiful friend. This is the end, my only friend. The end of our elaborate plans. The end of everything that stands. It hurts to set you free, but you will never follow me—the end of laughter and soft lies. At the end of nights, we tried to die".Omg, this shit was dark! I need a way out. HELP ME!

"Let this ugly beast take me to Hell with it!". Mentally and physically exhausted, I felt like my life was over and hopeless. Tears streamed down my face as I thought about how devastated my mother would be if I ended my own life. Suddenly, excruciating pain shot through my stomach, and before I could even stand up, I Shit my pants and sat there crying as it ran down my legs and the patio furniture. Thankfully, no one was around as I stripped down and hosed everything off. With no end in sight, all I could do was pray in desperation as I sat on the toilet, wishing I could erase the last six months of my life.

My gastrointestinal system finally decided to give me a break. As I changed into clean clothing, I noticed a medicine cabinet. Glancing at my defeated expression in the mirror, the little monster suddenly said, "Hey, check out the medicine cabinet and see what's inside." I opened it up, but I found only an old bottle of Tylenol that had been sitting untouched for years. Feeling dejected, I shuffled out of the bathroom and into the kitchen. After pouring a glass of water, I plopped down in the chair typically occupied by Dina's dad and switched on the TV to distract myself. The news was looping endlessly as I took a sip of water; it felt like razor blades were slicing through my throat and stomach from the pain. Looking up at the television set in the bookcase, I observed the always depressing ass daily news.

I saw a lazy susan pushed up against the table out of the corner of my eye, and realized that it was filled with prescriptions for her father. The same kind of ray had in Lexington. There were about twenty-five pill bottles containing medications for blood pressure, cholesterol, urinary issues, and prostate problems. When I thought all hope was lost, I noticed one bottle with the magical sticker I had hoped for: " May cause drowsiness, do not drive or operate machinery." "Bingo!" the little monster screamed. I grabbed it from the lazy susan and read the Lortab 10/750 label. Take as needed for pain. To my delight, I found twenty-one pills left from the original script of thirty written in 1998!

These pills had been there for almost two years, and I counted that he had only taken nine of them. That left 21 out of the original 30 prescribed. That meant two things; both were beneficial to me. Number one: He hadn't taken any of them in a very long time, and number two: I was sure he wouldn't miss a few pills. As I contemplated how many I should take, the little monster spoke up quickly and told me, "Take them all!" I knew if I didn't act now, I'd never be able to bring myself to do it. So, with haste, I grabbed the entire bottle and shuffled the other bottles around in the lazy susan to hide its absence. Racing back to the kitchen, I filled a glass with water and downed 11 pills as quickly as possible, then returned outside to sit by the pool.

The fears and worries that had consumed me 15 minutes ago slowly faded away as the effects of the hydrocodone kicked in. Sitting in the sun felt like I was wrapped in a cocoon of love, peace, and tranquility. Everything seemed perfect. Why couldn't I turn back time and feel the way I did before my car accident? Had my previous 36 years of life been an illusion? Was happiness now only achievable through pills? Then suddenly, a wave of dopamine hit me, and a tiny voice inside my head said: "We will always have good times, Jimmy, don't worry! The negative thoughts had been extinguished! Don't worry, Jimmy, be happy!"

" Do all tunnels really have light, or does our imagination always see the end."

James Powers

Chapter 25

Back In the Saddle Again

The rest of that afternoon went by great. I lay in the sun until Dina and her parents came home, and her dad cooked one helluva Greek dinner. I somehow saved the remaining ten pills and took them the following morning when I awoke. Everyone was gone again to work, and I worked on my tan for the second day. About mid-afternoon, the little monster reared his ugly head from his cave and started the same malicious rant he always did. "I need some damn pills. Whatcha gonna do? I couldn't give him an answer, and this dead-end didn't sit well with him. "You need to call Billy, you dumbass. Anyone that can get that pure cocaine should be able to get some damn puny pain pills," he told me.

I dialed Billy's number, and he answered the first ring. "What's going on, brother," I said in the most enthusiastic voice I could muster. "Not much, "he replied. "Hey man, do you know anyone who can get pain pills, like Lortab, Percocet, or even better, OxyContin?". " Not really, but let me make a few calls, and I will get with you after work," he said. Sounds good, man, much appreciated." I will call you later. It was already about 4 o'clock, and the very beginning of withdrawal had started, or at least it had in my head! I didn't feel very well, and the little monster reminded me that the rodeo was fast approaching opening night! Billy called me back and said he couldn't find any pills, but he put the word out. He also told me most of his buddies in his circle mostly smoked weed and snorted blow. This would not help me at all, I thought. Then I stashed that bit of knowledge in my big Rolodex of drugs and dealers in my mind! I ate dinner again with Dina and her family and went to bed reasonably early, already in the throes of starting to withdraw. I went to bed with all these terrible thoughts running around in my head about what tomorrow will bring. I took a considerable dose of Nyquil, and off to sleep I went. The dream started as always. A doomed jet doing a death spiral towards the ground, then a hangar filled with caskets floating in this bloody river of limbs and arteries that flowed on the floor danced in my head. The end of the dream was always the same as well. I would wake up in a pool of sweat. So, guess what happened this time? I woke up in a pool of sweat in my bed.

Wow, I felt like shit. My head was banging, my stomach was whirling like a blender, and every pore in my body seemed to protrude with these cold sweat bead bullets, smelling of sour, fruit-acidic rot. My feet had barely hit the floor until, well, you guys know by now, the little firefighter's hose was packed full, and we would release it in a fraction of a second. I ran to the bathroom and luckily made it in time for the mini-nuclear explosion that erupted out of me. I sat there in total despair, and the entire time, the lil monster was screaming his now too-familiar rant, "What the fuck you gonna do, Jimmy?! I need some pills, and I need them now!" Sitting there contemplating what I would do, the world was caving in.

In my entire time on this narcotic ride, I had never been more depressed than I was at this very moment. It was close to noon, and I knew Dina and her parents would be home in hours. I looked and felt like I would not make it this time. I was so exhausted mentally and physically at this point that death sounded like my best option. I wasn't strong enough to beat this beast anymore! He had worn my ass out, plain and simple! You win motherfucker, I give!, he had won, I thought. As I sat on the toilet, the tears were streaming down my face, thinking about what I had done to my life! I just wanted to forget! I just wanted to return to the way things were before the wreck. Please, God, could I have just one do-over, just one time?" my crippled mind thought. Unfortunately, I couldn't. This was my reality and life now! Fuck it, I thought, as I stood up and pulled my underwear and shorts up! Fuck this shit; I'm tired of feeling like this. It's time not to feel a damn thing, my mind thought. It's time to end this pain and torture! I walked into the kitchen and started opening drawers, looking and knowing the quickest way to not feel like this anymore. The first drawer was of big-ass kitchen butcher knives; ouch, I thought as I closed the drawer back. I never understood how someone could take a knife and commit suicide! That shit would hurt BAD, I casually thought. Hanging would suck too seriously, snapping your neck, hanging there, and choking to death while your eyes are trying to burst out of your face spontaneously. Like those images, we have all seen when someone gets strapped into the electric chair and their eyes explode and slowly drip down their face in this gross-ass jelly substance!

No, I thought all those methods seemed painful and unnecessary if you were going to bail! I had always thought the best way would be just to OD on the drug of your choice. Being in that euphoric land of Oz and just nodding out sounded much better than any other methods I had heard of, but today would not be that day. This I knew! I damn sure didn't have an entire bottle of pills to OD on! And if I had a whole bottle of pills, I sarcastically, then comically thought, my mind definitely wouldn't be in a withdrawing deadly state of mind, that's for damn sure! I would eat those motherfuckers like popcorn kernels and enjoy the ride, that's for damn sure! No, I knew exactly how to end this feeling, and it didn't involve dying today either, which was a good thing! I thought the phonebook had to be in one of these drawers. "Bingo, "I said out loud as I found the relatively thin phonebook in a drawer by the TV in the kitchen. Let's see a, b, c, d, e, f, g; I repeated BINGO aloud. As I let my fingers walk in the yellow pages under the letter H, finding the first hospital listed didn't take long. It was less than 5 miles away. I could be out of this misery when Dina and her family got home for dinner tonight. I hurriedly grabbed my keys, smokes, and lighter and hopped in my car. Next stop, Dilaudid Drive! I turned the ignition and started my 10-minute journey to the stars!

I had a searing stomach pain as I pulled into the parking lot, so I thought this would help my performance. The closer I got to the emergency room door, the slower I walked and the shorter I became from starting to bend over in pain. I walked into the emergency room, and my heart sank as I saw folks wall-to-wall waiting. I almost turned around to leave, but the little monster in my head said, "What in the hell are you going to do if you leave? Go home and let everyone see you in this shape"? He was right. I was in terrible shape in every way imaginable!

I walked through the double door and began moaning and crying out, "I'm dying, I think. I'm in so much pain". I bent over and said nothing, just moaned the same thing over and over: "Please help me," please help me, over and over! The two doors leading back to the treatment rooms swung open. A nurse with a wheelchair rolled right up to me and said, "Do you need help to get into the wheelchair?" "No, I believe I can. I gingerly tried to stand completely up and get in the wheelchair while convincing my audience I was really in this detrimental pain. "My side is on fire. It feels like I have a butcher knife stuck in me," I said. "Don't worry, sir, we are going to take care of you," the nurse said. "Thank you so much, mama," I painstakingly said. As I'm writing this, a feeling of total shame and guilt is rushing over me. Someone they put me in front of probably really was in a lot of pain and needed help a lot more than a pill addict withdrawing! I'm so ashamed of my actions when I was in the grip of this monster called pain pill addiction, but like I said earlier, If I was going to write this book, I was going to write it all, the good, bad, and ugly and this was an ugly part.

There is a lot of shame after addiction, this searing pain in your brain that is constantly reminding you of every shameful thing you ever did while this beast was inside of you. It's a process to forgive yourself! I've found it's much easier for folks to forgive you before you forgive yourself. I sincerely apologize to everyone I ever slighted in all the ERs I visited and everyone who truly needed help. I was a sick, self-centered monster, that's for sure! The nurse rolled me back to a bed, and I again did an Academy Award performance acting and made it seem like I could barely get up on the bed. After I got on the bed, I curled up in a fetal position and started moaning again about the pain I was incurring.

"Are you allergic to any medications?" she asked. "No, mam," I responded. "What in the hell do you think is wrong with me?" I asked her. "I think you have a kidney stone," she replied. "PERFECT," My twisted-up mind thought, this is too easy. "I'm going to put an IV in you so we can administer your medication," she said. Rufus strummed the first chord of "TELL ME

SOMETHING GOOD" and then came out on the stage in my mind and started singing his tune of "Tell me something good, aw tell me, tell me, tell me, tell me that you like it... yeah". I almost started laughing when I heard this. I was a sick motherfucker, that was for sure, but at least the sense of humor running around in my mind was still alive. At least I could still laugh as I moaned, realizing I had just about laughed! I noticed the nurse was on her way back, so I returned to my act of pain and despair. "OK, she said, I'm going to put this IV in your arm so we can administer your medicine." Tone Loc pushed Rufus off the stage and announced, "LET'S DO IT"! She gingerly slid the needle into the middle of my left arm, taped it down, and said, "OK, I'm going to start by giving you two medications." she said. "OK," I responded. "The first is a medication called Phenergan. It's for nausea. The second is Dilaudid; it's for pain. The little monster in my head started whooping, hollering, and doing the best happy dance he ever had!" OK, thank you," is all I could muster. She injected the first medication, and it felt cold going into my vein. She placed a cap on the used needle, threw it in the disposable needle bin, and uncapped the second one. The one that contained the solid rocket booster fuel that would blast and propel me out of these damn withdrawals and give me a nonstop flight to the orbits above. I watched intently as she uncapped the Dilaudid and began slowly pushing it into my mind, body, and soul. It initially felt warm, like a cup of cocoa on a blustery winter day. Like that warm bowl of chicken noodle soup, your mom made you when you were a kid, and you were sick! Just a whole body of warmth and a feeling of complete fulfillment and enlightenment!

About 5 seconds after the initial warmth, ground control took over. It began the blastoff. "commencing countdown engines on, check ignition, and may god's love be with you," Mr. Bowie reminded me! I immediately came out of withdrawal and feeling like shit and began feeling like a god, no, not a god, THE GOD! My rocket ride had begun, and Elton said, " Rocket man, burning out his fuse up here alone. "

Oh my god, it felt better than any other time I could remember. Fuck, this felt fantastic, mind-blowing, orgasmic! As always, The little monster told me, "Jimmy, don't worry, I got you; everything is going to be just fine," as always, I wholeheartedly believed him and believed everything would be just fine. "How's your pain, Mr. Powers?" the nurse asked. "my mind asked me quickly. "? How did she know your name?" and for a moment, I thought the gig was up. They had somehow figured out my diabolical scheme., I was in some fictitious kidney stone bank of names that the hospitals shared. That the lil monster quickly disregarded, saying, "Fuck 'em if they do, we got the juice"!. "How did you know my name? I inquired. You gave me your wallet and ID when you first came in. Here, you can have it back", she said. "Oh, I had completely forgotten," I casually replied. "How's your pain level now on a 1-10 scale, ten being the highest". "It was like 12 when I arrived. I think now about an 8, but that shot didn't help that much. It still hurts terribly so that I would say about an 8". "OK, she replied, I will get you some more medication," Rufus returned with his encore of "Tell me something good." "OK, thank you very much," I said. "You're more than welcome, Mr. Powers; I will be right back.".

As I lay there blasting through the planets and galaxies, my mind was in a good, mind-blowing space. Yeah, I had fucked up my life pretty severely, but what choice did I have now? Unlike

Memorex tapes, you can't push a button and rewind life! I could pull the trigger and end it, but no, this wasn't and had never been an option because of my mother. It would simply destroy her. She would probably die or go insane for the rest of her life, wondering what she could have done. I would never, ever do that to her, never! No one could do anything for me but me! I sometimes wonder if I hadn't had the mother god so graciously allowed me to have, would I have ended my life? I very well could have! In my life, I hadn't called out to God or followed the bible as I do today. My mom had always tried to keep me involved in church when she could, but unfortunately, I wasn't with her most of the time growing up.

My father raised me during those precious years of becoming a man, and he never went to church. Which, as I look back, is strange to me because my grandmother was there every time the doors were open, Literally! I remember as a kid always seeing bibles, crucifixes, and bible paraphernalia laying all around the house, and in some subliminal type way, I believe, helped lead me in the right direction later in my life. He thought I knew because later in life, when I would tell him I was going to church, he would always say without missing a beat, "Say a lil' prayer for me, Podge," and I always did and still keep him in my prayers today. I hope when the heavens judge him, God gives him a lot of credit for being a wonderful dad because he was a wonderful father, and I so miss him!! "Mr. Powers, are you awake?" the nurse asked. Damn it, I thought, I nodded out. "Yes, mam, it helps my pain a bit when I close my eyes," I said. That was the best I could come up with. I hope she believed me. My eyes widened when she uncapped the second Dilaudid rocket ride. I was getting ready to go on, though. You can bet your ass on that.

"I'm giving you some more Dilaudid for your pain," the nurse casually said. "Just keep 'em coming," the lil monster said. "OK, thank you, mam! "I will be back in about fifteen minutes to see how you're doing," she announced as she capped the second syringe of solid rocket booster fuel and threw it in the used syringe bin."Now it's time to leave the capsule if you dare; this is significant tom to ground control. I'm stepping through the door, and I'm floating most peculiarly," Mr. Bowie reminded me. The nurse returned in 15 minutes and asked the famous question I would hear thousands of times on my fifteen-year ride. "How's your pain level now, Mr. Powers?". "BE CAREFUL AND ANSWER THIS CORRECTLY," The little monster insisted, in a calmer voice than usual. "I still sorta feel a bit of a stabbing in my lower side, " I said. "Well, I have given you a lot of pain medication". That was another line I would also hear repeatedly in my fifteen-year ride! "Let me ask the doctor if I can give you more." You guessed it: ANOTHER line I would listen to over and over from nurses in my fifteen-year addiction. "Just get it and shut the fuck up" The lil monster put his 2 cents in as always. "OK, thank you, mam!. About 5 minutes later, I saw her coming, but my thoughts got watered down just for a moment because I didn't see her carrying the lil magical cylinder with the rocket fuel. "Oh well, my narcotic soaked sponge of a brain thought had already surmised, that sucks. "OK, Mr. Powers, the doctor has allowed me to give you one more shot of Dilaudid before you go," she announced as she magically pulled a syringe out of the front pocket of the apron she was wearing." WHAT?? FUCKING A!!! "I laughingly thought of a magician pulling the famous rabbit out of his black top hat. Elton returned on stage as she plunged the magical elixir into my vein. "I'm not the man they think I am at home. Oh no, no, no…I'm A ROCKETMAN. I was the fucking Rocketman right now, baby, that's for sure! OK, thank you so much," I pushed out. About 15 minutes later, she came back and announced, "We are going to take you for a test to locate the kidney stone, "Oh shit, how am I gonna deflect this, I thought, AND without hesitation, I just blurted out, "I can't take the test I'm allergic to the dye"! The next sentence out of her mouth scared the shit out of me for some strange reason. "How did you know it involved die"? Oh, fuck, fuck, fuck my gelatin-like, slowly processing mind thought. "OK, Jimmy, process and think, process and think," The lil monster urged me on," don't fuck this up"! As always, my quick-acting response was perfect, or at least that's what my fucked up brain was telling me anyway, and I believed it.   Remember I told you I had a kidney stone once before, "I informed her. ' Oh, I don't remember you telling me that," she acknowledged. "I'm so sorry, I thought I had," I responded innocently, and I saw it on her face: she had bought it. She had swallowed it hook, line, and sinker and never missed a beat after that. "OK, I will be right back," she said. She returned about 10-15 minutes later with many instructions, but honestly, all I heard was, "The Doctor has written this prescription for Percocet for you." Thank you! This is again all I could say as I signed the paperwork and levitated towards the exit. "You're not driving, are you, Mr Powers?" I heard the nurse ask from behind me. "No, mam, I'm waiting for my ride to come," I said as I walked around the corner to the bottom of the parking lot where I had parked. I learned quickly not to park near where they could see you leave!

"There is nothing permanent except change."

Heraclitus

Chapter 26

Here, Kitty, Kitty, Kitty

I returned to Dina by dinner time and was higher than a Georgia pine, but no one knew. When I asked her later in life if she or her mom or dad had a clue, I was blasted out of my mind on morphine during that dinner. Dina said, "No one had a clue. You looked fine to me.".

I went and filled the 20 Percocets the afternoon I left the hospital, so the next couple of days were OK but not great! The Percocets didn't give me that high that OxyContin did. Honestly, nothing gave me the high OxyContin did now that I look back and explore my 15-year odyssey: NOTHING, ZERO, NOTTA! Those oxys were the shit! Often impersonated but never duplicated. I knew a guy that has done the best white dragon heroin on planet Earth. Which is by far the best heroin I have heard from guys that would know. Trust me! Pure heroin, I mean 100% pure heroin.

A very close friend told me that it only existed in the fields of an area called the Golden Triangle. My buddy was lucky enough to be a free spirit back in the day, did some backpacking in a few of the

Golden Triangle areas, and got his hands on some straight from the jungle processor. He had stayed a week with a guy in Myanmar, Burma. The guy's uncle was a significant poppy grower and had a processing plant deep in the jungle of Myanmar. My buddy backpacked for two days to reach the processing plant buried deep in the jungle. The Golden Triangle is a geographical area that borders China, Thailand, Laos, and Myanmar. It is an area that covers 950,000 square kilometers of the best poppy grown on planet Earth and the only place I was told where the "PURE" white lady heroin is produced. You must be lucky enough to get it on its first stop out of the jungle. He told me if you gave him equal amounts of either to do that, he would take the oxy EVERY single time. It was a synthetically produced narcotic in its purest form. Made and controlled in a laboratory by a cast of the most brilliant guys in the world in their respective fields who wanted to make the most potent narcotic ever made, and it ended up being a helluva lot worse, and they succeeded!

The comparison between an 80 mg oxy and 8- 10mg Percocet was like comparing a Lamborghini Countach to a

Volkswagen rabbit. There isn't any comparison. The guys at Purdue Pharma created a monster and set it loose in modern-day society without regard. In 2021, the United States Supreme Court found the Sackler family would not be liable and or able to be sued in opioid cases. However, they forced Purdue Pharmacy to go bankrupt and pay approximately 4 billion dollars in restitution to the towns and communities they had helped destroy. They made about 31 billion on sales of OxyContin, so spending a 4 billion dollar fine was only about 13% of the actual revenue they made. Merely a proverbial "slap on the wrist"!

If you haven't watched a series on Hulu called Dopesick, I highly recommend it. It's a 100% Accurate account of what Purdue Pharma and the Sackler family did in the most susceptible small rural counties in the poorest communities, especially in the Appalachian area of the United States, Eastern Kentucky in particular. The small rural towns where folks worked their asses off, backbreaking work, working in coal mines. They unleashed this shit on folks who were already in pain and marketed this beast as a MIRACLE: NON-ADDICTIVE CURE for all their pain. They knew every person working in those mines was in some pain. I can only imagine the middle-aged family man going to work in those mines every day to support his family in tremendous pain, and the first time, he took one of these little demon seeds and felt all that pain go away. Of course, they thought it was a miracle drug!! Again, perfect folks to set this beast loose on! This hits home with me because, of course, I was born in Kentucky. I have been down to Pikeville and met some excellent, down-to-earth Christian people who worked these backbreaking jobs daily to support their families, only then for a major corporation to come in and release this life and family-destroying monster into the entire community! They should put everyone who had a hand in making and approving this beast to be turned loose in our society in a giant mouse maze, inject oxy into their veins until they are tragically addicted, then tell them all to go home and deal with it. Without a nickel in their pockets! Man, this subject pisses me off! However, the Sackler family made billions and billions of dollars (31 BILLION IN SALES OF OXYCONTIN ALONE) from their Frankenstein-like invention of OxyContin and remains one of the wealthiest families in the United States! They could and should go down in history as the biggest and most profitable drug cartel in planet Earth's history! Period, amen! Sorry, I went off there for a minute. This subject raises my blood pressure a bit. Those greedy cocksuckers!!

OK, so where were we? The only thing Percocet or Lortab were good for anymore was staving off withdrawals and keeping the lil monster locked up in his cage. They were a godsend, as if there was nothing else available. However, that mind-blowing euphoric feeling I had felt with that first bottle of Percocet was long gone. That particular space in my head was getting harder and harder. It was still there; getting the door open took a little more prying.

I only had about 7 Percocets left when Billy called and said, "Hey man, I'm heading out to my buddies to take him a lil' something.". I was going to ask him about what you had inquired about. "You wanna get outta the house a while and ride with me?" asked Billy.   " Fucking A, I do! I need to get the hell outta here awhile". My week-long vacation by the pool was getting old! In a joking manner, I laughed and expressed my need to escape from here in multiple ways. I needed to go out and make new connections, no doubt about it. In addition, I needed a new job to purchase supplies from potential new connections. I needed a lot of things right now, I thought.

"OK, man, I will be down to pick you up in about 10 mins". "Sounds good, brother; see you then," I responded. "This guy we are going out to see is Dina's uncle," he said after our brief journey began. "Huh? What the fuck" I thought, "Is he cool? "I asked. "Yeah, he's fucking crazy, but cool." The whole family knows he is out there. He is a very cool dude who likes his Crank," he laughed. "Crank, what the hell is crank" I asked innocently? Hell, I don't know, it's just called Crank," you snort a line and can do whatever, you're doing and be more intensely into it, or work your ass off for 24 hrs. You feel great." "Like blow?" I asked. "Yeah, and no sorta," Billy said. "You get high, like from the blow, but it lasts a lot longer and doesn't make you as paranoid. "So why do you blow?" I asked. "Crank seems to bend your mind up a lil more after doing it a couple of days.", Billy said. "Cool" was all I could think of to reply.

I got the idea from his answer that the end of a crank ride must have been pretty bad!! It could never be as bad as withdrawing from opioids, though my mind thought! Those reading this probably have heard of Crank or have some loose interpretation of what it was.

It has been replaced in the drug hierarchy evolution today as methamphetamine or Ice. Crank an older name for meth. Motorcycle gangs used to transport it and smuggle it in the crankcase of their motorcycles, hence the name crank. Crank was some nasty ass shit, though. Take it from someone who has had a taste of them all. If you were to take 10 percent of the purest form of crystal meth or Ice, cut it with 90 percent of every nasty ass thing you have ever heard that they missed any powder drug with, and mix it all together, you would get the old-fashioned Crank. Just simply some nasty shit!

We pulled up to this farm entrance, drove back a little lane for about a quarter mile, and drove to a decent house. Byron came out and met us in the driveway as we exited the truck. "What's up, my brother? Billy excitedly said. "Not much, just movin' and shakin', movin' and shakin'.", Byron replied as he did some weird ass crank-inspired ritual dance. I would come to find out by being around a few of them so-called crank heads in the next few years that this crank shit would fuck you up! Not only while you were ingesting it, but FOREVER! I met several guys who twitched uncontrollably or acted like someone with a severe case of Tourette Syndrome.

It scared the shit outta me, and again, I didn't scare easily back then. Any drug that was going to make you have uncontrollable nervous twitches in every part of your body for the rest of your life would end up making you dumb and weird. I met some dudes who would make some of Jack Nicholson's friends in One Flew Over The Cuckoo's Nest look like a congressional representative. Some weird ass mofos, that's for sure!

"This is Jimmy, Dina's friend from Kentucky."Billy continued." Nice to meet ya, man," Byron said. Byron rattled it off so fast that I had to rewind it in my mind for a time or two. "You as well, my brother," I said. "Y'all come in and take a load off," Byron said. As I walked in, I suddenly got it. I now understood the outside of the house was a facade but in decent shape, but when you walked inside, it was a bachelor pad of a dude that liked crank A LOT. Byron wasn't a filthy hoarder, like on the TV show. Just a lot of shit lying around in odd places and a ton of drug paraphernalia EVERYWHERE! ".

I came to know Byron reasonably well in the next couple of years, and deep inside, he was a great standup dude. Life threw Byron several nasty curveballs, and he responded the best he knew how. Deep down, though, he was a great dude! "Here ya go, brother! "Billy announced as he threw a small baggie of white powder across the table to Byron. "Thank you, sir," Byron replied in a millisecond as he hastily shoved the little baggie in the side pocket of his jeans. "Hey man, you know anywhere Jimmy could get some pain pills?" Billy asked! Please, please, please let him say yes, the lil monster said from deep within. "No, not really."

FUCK, I thought. "Maybe, though?" Byron continued, and my ears perked up! "I know this one, dude. I will reach out to him tomorrow. He's working right now," Byron said. The lil monster did not like this answer! "Tomorrow's ass," the lil monster said, "Fuck that, we need them now. Tell him to call him at work. Tell him, Jimmy. NOW DAMMIT!!! "the lil monster screamed.

"Thanks, brother. I will check back tomorrow." I didn't want to seem too desperate. However, the little monster was right; we needed them now! "Hey, man, have either of you ever done any shit called "Special K'?" Billy asked. "No, I haven't," I chimed in. "Aint that shit for cats? "Byron jokingly added in. I burst out in laughter! He was just one of them, dudes, that anything he said was sorta funny, AND when he answered, "Ain't that shit for cats?" I busted out in laughter! "I don't know," Billy said as he laughed.

"A buddy of mine traded me a lil' bag for some blow. You guys wanna do a line?" Billy asked. "Hell yeah," Byron answered as quickly as if he were answering the last question in his favorite category on Jeopardy! "Sure, why not," I said. "Got a mirror, Byron?" was Billy's next question. "Just pour that shit out on the table!" Byron exclaimed. The kitchen table had a glass top. I remember laughing and thinking how convenient it was. "Fuck it, let's do it," Billy announced. He pulled out the lil baggie from his pocket and opened it. Billy poured some of the white powdery substance out on the table. "Loosen that hand up a lil bit there, bud."Byron laughingly jokes, but he wasn't joking in reality. "You don't do this shit like a blow,"

Byron said. "My buddy said you wanted to do about a quarter the size of a normal line you would do, if even that much, "Billy finished. "He just must be scared." Again, another funny line from Byron. "Fuck it then!" Billy responded, turned the small baggie upside down, and emptied all its contents on the table. It was a good, solid gram, I know. "Just cut out whatcha want and get on it," Billy said.

I wasn't about to go first because I did not know what this would do to me and thought, let someone else go first. Before Billy had finished his sentence, Byron had kneeled by the table and cut out three huge ass lines, even by blow standards. Big Ass lines, trust me, ring finger lines! "I ain't doing that much of that shit," Billy said." Well, watch me," Byron said and bent down to the table, rolled up a dollar bill, and snorted the fattest line on the table. "Your gonna get fucked up," Billy said. "And I love it," Byron responded. "Go ahead, Jimmy," Billy said. "You can go, brother," I answered quickly back.

"Why don't you cut us out two regular lines, and we will do them," I said. Billy bent down and took one of the two remaining lines left, cut it in half, and then in half again, so in reality, we're doing a quarter of the amount Byron did! "Awwwee, big pussies, snort it all, "Byron said. Of course he said this, I thought. I Don't think he realized he might do this trip in his Special K orbit! He did now, though! "Fuck that," Billy said as he snorted the baby line and passed me the dollar bill, and I finished it. He poured the rest back into the bag, and we continued talking.

The next part will be easy to understand if you have done "K" before, but if not, I'm going to use my best to articulate what this shit did to us. We continued talking as Byron went to the kitchen and grabbed a glass of water. No soda, no beer. WATER, of all things, was the main staple in Byron's house. I doubt Byron was healthy and staying on top of his hydration. I guess it was the easiest option. He returned and sat the glasses down, and suddenly, I felt this slow-motion feeling in my mind and physical body. Billy looked at me, and I swear I could read his mind. "Man, he is going to be fucked up, I mean bad" Billy mentally transported this thought to my mind at the same time I did him. "YES, HE IS," I subconsciously sent back my telepathic answer.

"Where is the bathroom at, brother?" I asked Byron. "Down the hall and to the right.". Cool, I responded. As I walked, suddenly, it felt like my feet were moving through a foot of partially set concrete. I knew they were watching me because they were quiet, something that RARELY happened. I would learn when this bunch got together, I promise you. "How ya feeling, big fella? " Billy asked. My answer was simple and to the point. "You will find out when you get up and try to walk. " I laughed out loud and continued my longer-than-normal walk to the shitter! I walked into the bathroom SLOWLY. VERY SLOWLY! This shit was weird, and honestly, I hated it, and I knew the ride had just begun. I had done some shit a couple of years back called GHB, which I had hated. I drug my feet in my flip-flops and almost tore two toes off when I did that shit. It made every function your brain was telling your body to do ten times more complex and slower; it was the worst drug I had ever done until this Special K shit!

My still semi-conscious mind said fuck it, just try to enjoy it somehow and get through it. I eventually got to the toilet, pulled my shorts and underwear down, and sat down on the toilet. When I sat down, it didn't feel right. It felt like I had sat on an inflatable ring slowly losing air. My ass felt like I had seated on a giant ass sponge full of water. I told myself to embrace the buzz and just get through it, and as soon as I had almost convinced myself, the lil monster screamed from his cave, "You stupid motherfucker you ruined the lil opioid narcotic buzz I was enjoying; gonna be fun withdrawing when you come down from this shit "the lil monster said. I knew exactly what he was saying; as usual, he was spot on! Well, now I knew I had absolutely zero chance of enjoying ANYTHING the rest of the time on this fucked up ride. I sat there for what seemed like an eternity and finally came up with the energy to stand up and pull my shorts and underwear back up. I tried washing my hands in the jelly-like water, dried them off on my shorts, and opened the door.

As I turned the corner back into the kitchen, Billy was sitting there with his head propped up by his right arm, and all he said was, "Man, I'm fucked up." ME TOO" is all I got out before my ass hit the kitchen chair beside him. " Where in the hell did Byron go?" I asked. "Don't know, man," he said. He needed to go out to the barn for a minute, and he would be right back. "Brother, He is going to be one fucked up duck," I said, as I sorta laughed. "You ain't a shittin'," Billy slurred back at me. Let's just wait a few minutes. I don't feel like walking very far right now. Me either.

We both agreed to set a few minutes and get our bearings together. Well, a few minutes certainly didn't help our current situation at all. My body had made small uncontrollable movements, like slowly shaking, like I was a molecule of water bouncing between ice cubes in an ice-filled cup. I looked at Billy, and it seemed we were instantaneously going through the same things and thoughts. "Bro, he just did four times the amount of K you and I just did," I said in more of a question than a statement. "He could die, bro," Billy said. I can't imagine doing a line of that shit that big". I can barely walk and or function right now," I continued. "You think you can walk out to the barn"? Billy asked. "Fuck, I don't know, but together we can try. We need to find him, bro. I'm a serious heart attack. Shit might kill 'em!"." Let's go," he said. We stood up and held onto each other like a couple of guys who had drunk from happy hour till the bar closed at 3 am would walk and hold each other up after an 8-hour binge at a bar!

It was only about 30 yards to the barn, but it seemed like it took us an hour to get there. "Man, I'm not a big fan of this shit, you? "Fuck no, who in the hell wants to feel like your body weighs a thousand lbs, and every lil movement seems like it takes all your energy outta you.", "NO shit, "I said. "First and last trip on this, shit," I said. "YES, SIR " Billy responded. We didn't see Byron anywhere as we turned the corner and walked into the barn. "Byron, where the fuck you at?" Billy yelled out. No response at all! I looked at Billy, and he looked at me again, and our telepathic thoughts agreed again. "He's lying dead somewhere," I said." Well, let's find his ass and figure it out," Billy said. This is the exact old country barn you would see in your mind's eye or movies. There was an old ass car that looked like it had not run in centuries and a tractor that looked like they used it daily. As we walked in front of the tractor, we saw nothing.

We continued walking over to the car, and all Billy said was, "What the fuck?". As I looked down, I saw two legs protruding about a foot in the car's front. Like if someone was under the car doing some mechanical work. "What the fuck are you doing, Byron?" Billy asked. My mind, for some strange reason as I always did, started hearing a song in my mind. This time, the old rock group Genesis called, "No reply at all." "Is anybody listening? Oh-oh, there's no reply at all"! Billy repeated his request and questioned louder, and said, "Byron, wake the fuck up." I bent down and picked up one of his protruding legs and then let it go. It felt like something attached to a dead man. "He's fucking dead, bro," I announced to Billy and repeated the leg drop one more time. "Let's pull his ass out from under the car," Billy said. We each grabbed a leg and started pulling. When we got to the face and just about had him completely out, I noticed his face looked like a new solid white sheet. My scrambled mind snickered and thought, "He damn sure was "white as a sheet." We got him completely out from under the front of the car, and he was lifeless. Billy smacked Byron's face pretty damn hard and NOTHING. Our telepathic-synched minds started dancing in a thousand different directions and thoughts, but they all came back to one simple question. "What tha fuck were we going to do? "What tha fuck are we going to do? "Billy asked. Neither of us could hardly walk, and Byron was lying there, dead. Billy had a pocket full of cocaine and Special K, and Byron's autopsy would show he simply had OD'd on Special K. This was a fucked up situation. "Hey man, you know how to check his pulse?" Billy asked. "Not really, but it can't be that hard," I replied. I placed my forefinger and middle finger together and placed them on Byron's carotid artery or where I thought it was from movies I had watched where they checked to see if someone was dead or alive. "Nothing, bro, I can't feel shit" The reply was short and 100% true; I couldn't feel any blood flowing through Byron at all. Billy stood up and yelled, "Fuck, Fuck, Fuck, Byron, I fuckin' told you not to do that much, you dumbass, and kicked his leg.

After he had said this and kicked his leg, we both heard this very faint gurgling type of noise and then it hit us both." He's fuckin' alive," we both said at almost the same time. Like a shot of adrenaline hit us both as we began trying to talk to him. We took turns methodically slapping his face, hoping for more consciousness from him. "You alright, man? Hey, Byron, you alright?" Billy repeated over and over. We got no response, but at least we knew he was alive. We both stood up simultaneously, and that's when the giant wave of "now I can't walk hit us. We both stumbled down on the ground, and now all three lay together in a row. I remember comically laughing inside and thinking about the Three Stooges! As I looked at the barn ceiling, Billy said, "I got this bad feeling he is going to die unless we do something." "What the Hell are we gonna do, bro? We can't even walk," I said, perplexed. Billy agreed. "I know, man, I don't know what tha fuck to do."

We all three lay there, exactly like the three stooges would have looked after they had hit each other upside the head with something and fell. "You think we should call 911?" I asked." And tell them what?" Billy responded. "That he snorted too much Special K and that we didn't do as much. That's why we can barely walk, and he died?" I let out an exaggerated sigh. Point, I see what you're saying. Guess we can just try to ride it out with him till he's coherent, I guess?" I wasn't confident, nor was I sober. "What if he dies, though, bro?" I asked." He ain't gonna die. If he was, it would have already killed him," Billy responded.

The solution came into my mind like a runaway freight train, or so I thought. Before the last word came out of his mouth, I thought and said out loud to Billy. "Hey man, you got some blow in your pocket, right?". Billy looked at me, puzzled. "Yeah, why?". "Think about it. Special K is a downer apparently, right? We both sort of chuckled, and Billy laughingly said, "Ya think" It's a fuckin' animal tranquilizer." We both laughed out loud as Byron continued making these weird ass noises. We had been at least smart enough to lay him on his side in case he puked so this airway wouldn't be blocked. I then dropped my brilliant idea. "I bet if we do a big ass line, it would counteract this shit some," I said. "That's a great fuckin idea," he announced enthusiastically! We continued laying on our backs as Billy pulled the baggie of blow from one pocket, methodically reached in the other, and pulled out a cut straw.

"I laughed as I announced, "You're a one-stop snortin' shop!.

"hell yeah," Billy responded. "Just push the straw into the bag until

it's full, and we will lie here and snort it on our backs. "Only way to

do it. I can't walk," Billy said. "Me either. I can barely stand up." I

snickered. Then, I watched as he filled the 2-inch piece of straw by

continuously tapping it into the bag. "You wanna go first?" he said.

"No, you go ahead, bro," I responded. I watched closely as he put

the very end of the straw up his nose and took his finger off the other

end, and made this deafening ass snorting noise. I watched in

amazement as he shook his head back and forth a few times and

slowly stood up. "You're a damn genius," Billy announced. "I feel

great now. "Well, load me up one of those lil bombs so I can," I said.

He repeated the steps, and so did I, and within 5 minutes, we both

were standing over Byron's lifeless body, freaking out about how to

handle this. "Fuck it, man, let's load one up and blow it up his nose,"

he said. "Ya know, it sounds crazy, but in theory, it just might

work," I said. Billy again repeated the cocaine shotgun ritual, handed

it to me, and said, "Blow it up his nose." Whoa, whoa, whoa, my

mind quickly thought. What if he OD's from it? "If we are going to

do this, I think we should both have a hand in it in case he dies, bro,"

I said. Billy didn't hesitate in saying, "You're right. OK, you tilt his head up a bit, and I will blow it up his nose". I gave Byron a shotgun bump, and Billy did as well.

About 30 seconds later, Byron started coughing and gagging. I honestly thought he was going to die, but he didn't. He simply shook his head 3 or 4 times and then stood up and said, "What the fuck happened?". Billy and I looked at each other again in sheer amazement and again telepathically decided to just tell Byron the simple answer. "You just passed out for a bit.

"OK, why are we in the barn?" Byron asked. "You don't remember you were showing me your old car," I said. He simply said without hesitation, "You like it?". "Nice ass car!" I responded, and we walked back to the house.

We didn't hesitate, walking directly to Billy's truck and telling Byron we would catch him later. "I will call my buddy for you tomorrow, Jimmy." Thanks, brother; it was nice meeting you. Billy and I said little as we went home, but again, telepathically, I knew we both were thinking. Thank god we got out of there and Byron was alive.

" Could the angel on your shoulder simply be the devil in disguise?"

James Powers

Chapter 27

Time flies when you are having fun (And Doing Pills)

It's true; time flies when you are in the middle of this addiction. Every day seems to last an eternity if you are looking for pills, but after you get them and get fucked up, the time flies. The hardest part and some of you out there will know this as well as me, is when you're withdrawing and waiting for either A. Pills to be delivered or B. Waiting on your dealer to call so you can go pick them up. Man, those minutes feel like hours, days! Especially when you're withdrawing.

I can remember waking up at 9 or 10 am. Withdrawing like a motherfucker and calling the dealer. He could only tell me he could meet me at 4-5 pm. What was I going to do for 6-7 hours while withdrawing? I wish I had a quarter for every time this same scenario played out, and I would go to some city park or remote area and sit in my car for hours, gagging, puking, running down to the corner store to take a shit. Those were some long ass days, and if you were lucky, he would show up somewhere near on time.

You would act as normal as possible, get the pills and eat a handful as soon as he drove away and stay there for the 30-minute blastoff period, and then leave like it was just a typical ass day. It Gives me chills and makes me nauseous just writing about those days. I honestly must be one tough ass guy mentally because I put myself through some unreal shit, that's for sure! I'm sure I'm not special, though; this I know, and we all feel or have felt like that at the end of this vicious cycle! This shits a motherfucker, man! I wouldn't wish this shit on anyone EXCEPT Purdue Pharma and the Sackler family! Those guys need a good dose of the reality of oxy addiction, trust me.

The next few years were honestly a blur now, looking back. After a bunch of trips to the ER in many cities and towns, I had it down to a science. There is no doubt that if I'm ever cast in a role that requires that entire scene, I will win an Academy Award. HANDS DOWN!

I got a job at the same pizza chain I had worked for in Lexington and started doing the same shit, just with a different cast of characters. Believe it or not, pills were cheaper in Florida, which was just fine by me. Lortabs and Percocets were the easiest to get, but oxys seemed elusive, and that was by far my favorite. I tried snorting Florida cut heroin a few times, but as earlier mentioned in the previous paragraph, NOTHING CAME CLOSE to oxys! Plus, with oxy, I knew I was getting PURE narcotic, with heroin, especially in a small country town. You never knew what the fuck you were getting, and that scared me. That shit had been stepped on more times than a Macy's Day parade! I hated needles, though, and believe to this day that mere fact alone inevitably saved my life! If I didn't have a severe needle phobia, this book would be buried with me six feet under somewhere, trust me. These pages would have never come to fruition.

I snorted everything, loved snorting, and loved it! To get one of those fresh 80s, crush it up and make one extensive ass line and snort it in one big whoosh. Well, it just simply didn't get any better, at least to this person with an addiction! It was my entire life for 15 years! I can remember just how damn good it felt, sitting here right now. I fucking loved it.

Still do! But I don't love it as much as I hate what it did to me. It destroyed my life, period, amen. You can't sugarcoat a turd, brother! It cost me everything I ever loved or cared for and my two daughters. I was watching them grow up from afar and their life progression, love, everything! Gone now. My only reprieve and my mother instilled this into me from a very young age, but my only reprieve is I went through this for a reason. My mother always told me, "Jimmy, everything happens for a reason, "I can only pray she was right! If just the tiniest bit of good comes from this book! If just one lost soul out there reads it and picks up anything from it, any small nugget at all that helps them survive this shit storm of pain pill/opiate addiction, then I can rest easier and believe that yes, "Everything happens for a reason!

Why did I not simply end up being a statistic? Another spoke in this giant wheel of death called addiction. Last year, there were a reported 106,000 deaths by opioid overdose. In 2001, there were 20,000. Why weren't there 20,001 in 2001? How and why did I escape the inevitable fate that awaited so many? Maybe one person will read this and get clean. I could accept this as my reason for addiction and be 100% satisfied! I stayed with Dina and her family for a couple of years. They were some of my most shameful years. I stole her dad's Percocet after they diagnosed him with cancer. There is and was no excuse for this wretched behavior.

This disease, again, is just simply a motherfucker! It makes you say and do shit you never even would think about in your right mind! It makes me sick to my stomach right now just thinking about it. I sincerely apologize for anything and everything I did, not only to Dina but to her entire family. They were, and I'm sure still are, the salt of the earth. You won't meet better people, and they took my ass in like family, and for me to do some things I did, again, just makes me sick to my fuckin stomach. Ok, I've cried and squealed enough! We all do some fucked up shit while in the devil's palm, that's for sure! These are the times when I'm feeling like this that I have to lean into my mother's famous words of wisdom, "Everything happens for a reason, Jimmy". If it took all my trials and tribulations to get to this point, then so be it, I guess! I'm done; let's get back to the rollercoaster ride! It's time to get ready to go down the biggest dip on the ride!

" The little monster lives in all of us, some of us just feed it more,"

James Powers

Chapter 28

The Man with the Plan and the Tropical Tan

I understood Byron better after becoming friends with him; I knew deep down that he was decent. Now that 20 years have passed, I appreciate and understand him even more. We all were on our roller coasters, and it's all so clear now that I'm 60 and so far removed from it. Each of us had experienced some trauma, and taking drugs was an easy way for us to laugh away our sorrows. My drug of choice was painkillers; Byron favored crank, and Billy indulged in weed and cocaine. It was as simple as that.

After getting to know Byron better, one day, he called me and said, "Hey Jimmy, I got this buddy you might wanna meet - his name is Rob." He continued in his usual fast-paced tone. "What is he like?" I asked. Byron told me Rob had a supplier of OxyContin. Excitement surged through me at the mere mention of the drug. "Are you serious? Call him now!" my inner monster demanded. Byron assured me he'd already vouched for me and that all I had to do was call if I was interested. "Thanks, brother," I replied before ending the call and dialing Rob's number immediately. It had been a while since I'd done or seen any oxys, and the mere thought of it sent electricity surging through my brain like rocket fuel. That ultra-high state of euphoria only lasted two hours when I accessed it from the ER, but now, even that was getting harder and longer to achieve.

The little monster in my head woke up and kept pushing me to get them, no matter what it took. I was too high to ignore him, so I called Rob to see if he could help. "This is Jimmy, Byron's buddy. He gave me your number and said you might know where I could get a few fresh watermelons. He said your patch was about ready to pick?" "Watermelons?" Rob sounded dumbfounded. Honestly, I don't know where it came from either. I didn't want to mention anything illegal over the phone, so I asked for watermelons instead. After this encounter, Rob earned the nickname "Melon Man."

"Uh, yeah, yeah," he said. I could tell it took him a few seconds to process what I was saying. "Yeah, I've got a few now and will have the full crop picked soon," he answered. "I'd love to pick up what you already have," I asked timidly. "Not many," he mentioned. Damn! Was he referring to 1 or 2? I thought to myself. "Maybe around 15-20, though," Byron continued. "He considers that not many? What did he consider a lot? GET THEM ALL!" the little monster in my head insisted. "I can come by, or we can meet and get however many you have right now before we make plans for more after you pick them," I suggested. "Sounds good to me," Rob agreed. "I just checked, and I have 20, and they are six bucks each," Rob said. "The next time you get more than 20, I can go down to 5 bucks each," Rob added. Slot machine noises were going off inside my head; an 80 mg oxy for 5-6 bucks, that's almost impossible! "I can meet you at Tropicana Park in about 30 minutes if you'd like," Rob

offered. "With bells on, my brother!" I answered with enthusiasm.

He chuckled, then told me to see him there and that he'd be in a

black Ford truck. Sounds good! We ended the call, and the little

monster was doing his victory dance in my mind when something hit

me; I didn't even ask what milligrams these pills were.

I was lucky to get either the 40s or 80s for 5-6 bucks each.

After all, they made them in doses ranging from 10 milligrams to

80mgs. I was determined to ensure that whatever I bought would be

worth it. Heck, 10-milligram oxy's were worth 5 to 6 bucks each! I

arrived at the park ahead of time to check the area out. As I did, a

sense of paranoia briefly flashed through my mind when I recalled

he said he drove a black Ford truck. Hadn't I heard somewhere that

the FBI used black trucks as undercover cars? That thought quickly

vanished from my mind when I focused on getting some oxy in my

veins. Sitting in an area with a few cars, I watched some mothers and

their children playing on the playground.

A wave of the deepest depression ever suddenly overcame

me as I realized I had given away those days with my children and would never get them back. There, at that moment, I felt like ending it all; tears streamed down my face, and I couldn't stop shaking and crying. I was on the brink of hyperventilating when a black Ford truck pulled into the park entrance. I frantically wiped my face and tried to compose myself. In about one minute, he'd reach out his window and ask if I was Jimmy. I answered in a comical-like Jim Carey fashion, "I am!" He said cheerfully, "Jump in, let's take a ride."

My mind wandered to an alarming conclusion: he was about to arrest me. Then, I shook my head and exited the car, approaching his truck. "Hey brother, what's going on? My name's Rob," he said, to which I replied, "Not much, man, I'm Jimmy. Byron said you wanted some oxys?" That question alone made me suspicious. If I said yes, I thought the next thing could be the handcuffs coming out. Frustrated, I asked him, "Rob, are you a cop, or do you work for any law enforcement agency?" Rob laughed. "No, I'm just a watermelon farmer, and I don't work for any law enforcement agency," Rob replied, then added with a chuckle. I love the watermelon line. The funny thing is, I live on a farm with several watermelon patches!"

What's with the watermelon line?" I explained it was just what came

to mind, and he praised me for being creative. He handed me an

unlabeled pill bottle and said, "Well, now that we cleared that up,

here ya go." Grateful but still suspicious, I thanked him as we both

laughed.

Through the orange-tinted glass, I saw the pills weren't round

- nothing like the 80mg Oxy I was used to. The little monster started

ranting, "What the hell are these?? Tell him thanks for wasting our

time, and he can stick whatever fake ass pills he's trying to sell us up

his ass! I poured a few into my hand - almost the same size and color

as a 10mg Lortab, but more oblong and a deeper blue, almost purple.

Despite my skepticism, I poured one out into my hand and noticed it

had OC stamped onto one side like all oxy pills I'd done before,

along with "160 mg'' on the other side. "Uh, what the hell are these,

Rob? I've never seen an oxy like this?" Rob replied with awe in his

voice, "These, my friend, are 160 mg oxycontin, the strongest

narcotic ever made by man"!

The word "Bullshit" flew out of my mouth before I had the

chance to think. He handed me a pill with "OC'' stamped on one side and "160 mg" on the other. Before I could ask him questions, he spoke. He explained that this was equivalent to two 80 mg oxycodone, and my brain quickly figured out that this meant an 80mg oxy was only costing me three dollars! All I could say in response was, "Wow." I told him I had never seen these before and hadn't even known they existed. He explained they had only made them about six months prior, and before that, the strongest dosage was an 80mg tablet.

"Do you still want them?" Rob asked. The little monster answered sarcastically, "Does a cat have an ass " and was screaming out in excitement, but I remained calm on the exterior. "Sure, why not," I said as I pulled out six freshly minted Andrew Jackson twenties. I handed him the cash. "Just be careful with these. They're really strong - one pill equals two eighty mg oxys," Rob warned. "No need to take a full one at once. Do you eat or snort it?" Rob asked me. "I snort them; I have a phobia of needles, thank god! "Good thing, too - if I saw any track marks, we wouldn't be doing business here," He continued. "Byron told me you weren't into mainlining, so that's good, 'cause I don't want to be held responsible for an oxy OD, so watch yourself closely, Jimmy - be very careful." His words struck me, and I realized this was the first time a dealer had lectured me about drug use. In hindsight, it seemed like a gracious gesture.

I could cut them up into two lines and save one for later. This idea made the little monster inside my head laugh hysterically. "Oh, sure you will," he said mockingly. "Let me know if you like them and want more," Rob said. "How many can you get?" I asked. "Don't worry about it; just let me know how many you need, and keep in mind that anything over twenty is five bucks each," he replied. "Ok, thanks a lot! I'm sure I'll be in contact soon," I said as I opened the door and returned to my car.

"Stop the car and get a cassette tape out," the lil' monster demanded. Yes, this was back in the day of cassette tapes. "Crush up one of those monster 160 mg dreammakers, and let's get rid of this sick feeling," he continued. I remember laughing. The lil monster was calling the pill a monster. Wasn't that the pot calling the kettle black? I decided to meet him halfway and stop at the store I had always used when I was going to get pills. The last time I used this store was because the little firefighter was forcing me to stop, but not this time! A smile from ear to ear eased its way across my face. No, this trip would be different. I would queue up Elton and join the "Rocketman" this time! My insides screamed with excitement and anticipation as my foot floored the accelerator. "Stop the car over and put in a cassette," the little monster inside me demanded. "Let's get rid of this sick feeling and snort one of those 160s NOW!" I told him to " Fuck off," and I stopped at the 7-11.

Flip - Flop, Hippity Hop, Off your rocker and over the top, life's a fiction and the world's a lie,

put on some creedence and let's get high!"

Stephen King

Chapter 29

Winner Winner Oxy Dinner

I stepped into the 7-11, and my friend Mr. Patel greeted me with his usual, "Hello, Himmy! What's going on today, my friend?" I responded, "Not much, brother, another day, another dime, trying to make it a dollar." His chuckle showed he found this amusing. He told me the restroom was open if I needed it, so that was my first stop when I walked in. He knew my first stop upon entering his store was always the bathroom. I loved that restroom because it only had one stall and a big deadbolt on the door. The lock was so secure that not even a SWAT team could get in while I was inside. After I left the restroom, one of two things usually happened. If I was withdrawing, I said a short goodbye and left or, if I had gone into the toilet, To snort pills. I stayed a while to buy lottery tickets and chat with Mr Patel. As soon as I entered the bathroom, I locked the deadbolt and then sat backward on the toilet to clean off the back top of the seat with paper towels.

I had discovered that the back of a toilet was the perfect place to crush oxycontin pills ceremoniously. I even started to call it "The Dance of the Oxy" in my head. I would put the pill in my mouth, roll it around my tongue a couple of times, and Wala, the time release coating would be gone, and we could commence " The dance."Inevitably, I would pull out my pill and break it in half. I then would break it into two equal pieces before throwing them into my mouth without a second thought. For those who don't understand, oxycontin is a time-release tablet. Usually, you would swallow the entire pill as prescribed, and the coating would slowly dissolve over 12 hours, slowly releasing an amount of the opioid, oxycodone. The thing that made these drugs so irresistible was how quickly you could take a massive quantity of oxycodone at once. Just lick the outer coating off, crush up the pill and eat it, smoke it, snort it, or shoot it all at once. I could suddenly get 12 hours' worth of medication in an instant. It felt great snorting two eighty-milligram oxy pills; the little monster rationalized," Do the entire 160; you better not do just half, be a waste"! You've done 160 mgs at once before". You guessed it, another conversation he won. Then the little monster inside my head spoke up: "Crush up the whole pill, and let's get this party started," he demanded!"Come on, man, take the other half; crush it up, and let's go! Think about it: you've snorted 2-80s before, you will love it, at least I know I will," he laughed. He hadn't used that tone of voice before - reassuring and calm. His words rang true, and as always, he won the debate. Like always, he won again!

I took the other half of the pill and laid it on top of the first before covering the powder with a dollar bill. Taking out my BIC lighter, I started crushing them until the pills were reduced to a fine powder. When I lifted the bill, an impressive amount of white dust was revealed. To check that it was what I expected it to be, I put a small amount onto my finger and tasted it – the taste confirming that it was indeed a 160 mg oxy pill. After chopping it up one last time with my credit card, I licked the edge and created one of the largest lines I had ever seen. It practically stretched from end to end on the back of the toilet!

I couldn't believe my eyes when I saw how much powder this pill had created. It was huge—the line stretched from one end of the back of the toilet to the other, and it was as thick as my pinky finger! I fished a dollar bill out of my wallet and rolled it up. I wondered if I could do the whole thing in one hit or whether I should split it into two parts. The little monster inside me scoffed at my caution and told me to man up, so I got down low and put the straw at the end of the line. Taking a deep breath, I sucked it all in through my nose in one snort. I will never forget that taste. Even while sitting here writing this book, I can taste that shit! It's burned in my taste buds forever and ever, trust me!

I released all the air in my lungs and snorted the line of oxy in one big inhale. It made me gasp for breath, and I nearly vomited. Then, I slowly sat down on the toilet, leaning slightly forward. After A couple of minutes, a wave of warmth spread throughout my body. My thoughts were suddenly filled with an assurance that everything would be okay; this was different from before because there wasn't even a speck of doubt left in my mind. For those of you who have never snorted 160 mg of oxy at once, it's hard to explain what it feels like. Just imagine the most joyous surprise moment you have ever experienced, amplified ten times, then squared.

Reflecting on the happiest moment of my life is not enough to express its full intensity. I've heard that near-death experiences feel like an ultimate bliss of unconditional love and pure nirvana. Count me in if the afterlife is more fulfilling than snorting a 160! I remember feeling nothing but pure joy and euphoria when I left that

7-11 restroom in Ocala, Florida. Even now, I still believe that was the best Buzz of my life — the closest sensation to how it would feel to experience God's love in Heaven. Right now, Heaven is located in a 7-11 store in Ocala, Florida.

As I stepped out of the bathroom, I felt better. Even the ER visits and injections of Dilaudid didn't measure up - for me, oxy made morphine feel like child's play! I understand much later why Oxycontin became and remains the most abused drug in America. It is, without a doubt, the most robust narcotic available. And if you haven't experienced its effects personally, thank God! Some have lost their lives or been hurt because of it, and to them, my heart goes out. The same people who released this monster into societies around the world failed to consider its consequences: countless young lives destroyed, along with their families. Those responsible will pay dearly. If not in this life, I guarantee they will in the next!

Alright, where were we? As I walked out of the bathroom, my thoughts, body, and spirit felt utterly liberated. I'd never felt such freedom before! In this ecstatic trance, nothing seemed hostile;

everything would work out for the better. This was a positive experience.

"How've you been, my friend? " Mr. Patel smiled as he asked me the question. "Everything's good," he answered before offering what sounded like a great idea. "I just got new rolls of lottery tickets an hour ago, if you want to try your luck? The most expensive scratch-off in all of Florida was twenty bucks back then; today, it might even be fifty or sixty bucks, I'm not sure. I bought twenty-dollar tickets, which was the amount I could comfortably lose, so usually, I'd only buy one or two—three max. I had just given Rob 120 dollars from the 200 I had in my account, and payday wasn't for a whole week yet. So now I had eighty dollars left for food and other expenses. "Well... let me think about it," I replied hesitantly. Then suddenly, inside of me, the little monster spoke out from his cave. "I'm feeling lucky!" he chirped. This was unusual for him; usually, he stayed quiet when I was high! But here he was, being surprisingly optimistic. "We can't afford too many," I told him quickly. "I only have eighty bucks left in our bank account."

"Just write him a check! He trusts you; he'll do it," he insisted. "Buy a full roll of them, man; don't be a pussy!" I considered his jest and wondered if this were something I would have to tolerate now constantly: this small voice in my ear anytime I wanted to do something. "Ask him, dude!" Now, the little monster started yelling in my head. I stuttered: "Can you maybe accept a check from me?" Without time to process the response, the little monster screamed, "GET A WHOLE FKN ROLL! GET A WHOLE FKN ROLL!". " Anything for you, Himmy," he responded." Do you think you could do $600 so that I can buy an entire roll of twenty-dollar tickets?" of course, my buddy," Mr. Patel laughed and called me a "high roller, big money man," and I chuckled along with him. I went to my car to grab my checkbook out of the glove box and walked back in. He got out a new roll for me, and I filled out the check to Mr. Patel for $600. Then, I inspected this monstrously large lottery ticket roll; it must have weighed ten pounds! I asked myself what on Earth I was doing buying tickets lottery tickets by the pound now! I pulled the tape off the end of the first ticket on the roll of thirty and started scratching eagerly. At this point, I was high as a kite; I hadn't even considered the repercussions of writing him a bad check.

Thinking of all the money I could make, I completely overlooked that my friend had trusted me to pay him back.How much have you won, buddy? " Just a hundred, but I still have 24 tickets left," I said enthusiastically. I am sitting here writing and can remember exactly how I felt. I simply felt like a god. Like I didn't have a care in the world, and I loved everything, and everyone loved me! I simply didn't have a care or concern in the world; I had just written a check that was a felony offense! I think a line in a famous rap song went " "Insane in tha dope brain". I knew precisely what that meant and felt like! I scratched about 15 more tickets with no winners. A few paid the original investment of 20 bucks, but that wasn't going to get to 600 bucks, that's for sure. I remember getting ticket 22 [my favorite roulette number]. I got the magical symbol I had been hoping and praying for: " You win all prizes on the card! I completely freaked out and started jumping up and down. Mr. Patel was jumping up and down, asking, "How much did you win Hiimmy " " All the prizes on the card" I said " very enthusiastically." how much total" he asked? I don't know, let me see, and I presumed my scratching position. Let's see, five bucks, five bucks, five bucks, five bucks. It then hit that ALL the spots were 5 bucks, and there were 20 spots, so my very high mathematical brain wasn't quite as fast, but 20 x 5 was a pretty simple calculation; it was another 100-dollar ticket. So I now had 280 dollars back from 22 tickets, so I was averaging approximately 14 bucks per ticket, and I invested 20 bucks a ticket, so the numbers pointed to me not being able to reach my bare minimum goal of 600 to pay Mr Patel back. " Fuck it, Jimmy," the lil monster said. " Keep on scratching; let's win some cash." " My initial euphoric rush had muted a bit, not much, but that instant, overwhelming feeling of euphoria was dulling by the minute, and that lil fucker knew it when he spoke up, and said," I have a great idea, Jimmy. Let's go into the restroom, snort another pill, then scratch the last eight tickets," he said. I thought that wasn't a bad idea. Heck, I had 19 more 160 mg oxys left. If I did one more would still have 18 left in the morning, I thought. "Okay, okay, I responded to him. Still, we will do a half or 80 mgs" . " Cool" is the singular word that came out of his mouth. I went back into the restroom and repeated steps 1-5. I snorted an entire 160 mgs once again. I know I know, I said I was going just to do a half pill or 80 mgs, but right after I had sucked off the time release coating and dried them off, the lil monster called me a big pussy again, right at the time I was crushing half the pill up and AGAIN he won the debate! " You got the shits, Mr. Himmy," Mr. Patel asked? I started laughing my ass off. I was the highest I had ever been in my life. I thought to myself, " I could probably actually shit in my pants and not realize if I did, then simply laugh my ass off! After I snorted that second 160, I went to another level! One that, until this very moment in space and time, I never knew existed! This feeling was overwhelmingly amazing! A feeling words could never do justice to! You could have the mainlining Dilaudid all day long; give me the 160 oxys every time! I began scratching lotto tickets again to no avail. I hit a couple of 20s and was down to the last three tickets! I had 320 dollars' worth of winners in one pile of tickets and ticket numbers 28,29 and 30 in another! The 320 plus the 80 I had in my bank account only equaled 400. I had written the rubber check to Mr Patel for 600! I was fucked and could care less. I felt invincible and felt that nothing anyone could say or do would affect me negatively. I scratched the 28th ticket, and again, not! " Fuck it, Jimmy, buy another roll," the lil monster said! " Fuck you and shut the fuck up," I said back to him. He wasn't going to win this debate, I tried assuring myself! Ticket number 29, scratch, scratch, scratch, nothing. first, 15 spots on the card, five spots to go. I have, and still have, a particular way I like to scratch off my lotto tickets. I have always scratched the number above the prize, and if the number matched, I wouldn't uncover the prize until I had scratched them all off. Then, I would scratch the winning spots to see what prize or prizes I had won. Scratch, scratch spot 16, notta! The same results with spot #17 and 18. I had two more chances on this ticket and one more ticket with 20 chances, and I needed at least 280 bucks to cover the 600-dollar check. I scratched spot number 19 on card number 19, and the number matched one at the top, so, in essence, a winner of at least 20 bucks. They never gave you less than you paid if you hit a winning number. I then scratched the 20th spot, and again, nothing. I returned to the winning spot, number 19, and began slowly and methodically scratching off the prize. First, the number 1, then the number 5, then the number 0, and two smaller zeros at the end. " 150 bucks," I announced to Mr Patel. " Good for you, my friend," he replied. So, with that ticket, I now had 430 dollars of the original 600-dollar investment and one ticket to scratch.

I scratched the last ticket with high expectations only to get to the previous spot, scratch it off, and realize it was just another non-winning ticket. " Shit, shit, shit," I said to myself internally. The 430 bucks plus the 80 in my account only equaled 510. I was screwed! I might as well have had nothing, 0 dollars, because either way, The check I had written Mr Patel would never clear! At that very moment, I thought I didn't care at all. I felt the best I had ever felt, and a cold check wouldn't make me feel any worse; almost nothing would, I thought, in this head space! " Give me your tickets, Himmy, and I will cash them for you, buddy. " "Sounds good to me," I responded. I handed him the nine tickets that were winners, totaling 430 dollars, and thought to myself, " Not too shabby!". I watched as he fed the tickets into the machine that validated them.

Everything looked and felt completely normal until he scanned the last ticket. He got this confused, perplexed look on his face that, in a split second, turned into the biggest smile I had ever seen from him. " My buddy, my buddy, OMG, my buddy," he said.

The last ticket you thought was for a 150 150-dollar winner was a fifteen hundred dollar winner." congratulations my friend! "You shitin me, right? "I ask? As fireworks started in whatever hemisphere I was now in, ' No, my friend when I scanned it,' he continued to explain in a very excited way. " That's AWESOME" WOW! " So instead of getting 430 dollars back, you actually get back 1780.00 dollars, my friend". "OMG, THAT'S GREAT!" I said back in the same excited voice he had been using! "I hope you gotta bunch of 100s in that safe," I said, chuckling. OH, I'm sorry, my friend. For any winner over 600 dollars, you must go to the Gainesville lottery headquarters to cash. " WTF, ARE YOU KIDDING ME?" I Screamed in my mind!." Let's snort a celebratory pill, Jimmy" the little monster intervened in our conversation. " SHUT THA FUCK UP AND LET ME THINK," I yelled back at him. " That sucks" I said. " Just think of it as a 1780.00 dollar 45-minute drive to Gainesville. "You're right; it's still crazy good!" I resigned. My mathematical mind came racing back, and I quickly realized it was almost a 40-dollar-a-minute ride! Yes, I would take that for the rest of my life. He started to put the tickets in an envelope when my mind devised a brilliant plan. It's the most brilliant yet, I remember thinking in my narcotic-soaked mind. " Tell ya what, Mr Patel ". 'I owe you 600 dollars, right? "Right," he agreed. You're a good man and have been good to me, and you've become a great friend! (sales 101, stroke the buyer's ego).

Although I wasn't lying deep down, he had become a good friend! You tear the check-up, give me 600 more cash, and I will give you the tickets," I said. That's just how fucked up I was at the moment. I'm offering a guy 580 dollars to take an hour's ride; WTF! I opened my mouth quickly to take it back or act like I was kidding, and before I could even get a syllable out, he said, " You have a deal, buddy." I will be right back. All I could do was stand there with my mouth wide open in surprise at what had come out of my mouth! Would you watch the front of the store for a minute? " he asked. Of course, my friend, of course. He returned just a minute or two later with 600 - 100 dollar bills and handed them to me along with the rubber check I had written him an hour prior. Thanks a lot, my friend," I said. " I gotta be going." " Take care, and I'm sure I will see you soon." " You as well, " he said as I proceeded to walk out the front door of my neighborhood 7 - 11 !!

" At first the addiction is maintained by pleasure, but the intensity of the pleasure gradually diminishes, and the addiction is then maintained by the avoidance of pain. "

Frank Tallis

Chapter 30

The Rabbit Gets Lost In The Hole

The day I met Rob, everything changed. I was now introduced to something I never knew existed. The most potent narcotic on planet Earth, literally! The difference between snorting an 80 and a 160 was fantastic! This is where my addiction truly spiraled, and I was close to death more times than I care to remember. I remember when I first snorted an 80. I knew it couldn't get any better, but it did, and now it exists in my mind! A new pleasure zone, the next level in my narcotic race to the moon! More devastating than anything else, though, is that the little monster was aware of what a 160 felt like and forgot nothing!

Believe it or not, up to this point, I had never got so fucked up I couldn't function. I had never nodded or seemed out of it. I know a lot of people with a substance use disorder say that or at least wanna believe it. Still, I went back and asked a bunch of folks who were around me during this timeframe. They all confirmed, "Yeah, sometimes you acted a little strange, but never sloppy fucked up! You were always sweating, though, even during the winter!" My tolerance at this point was simply monstrous, Godzilla-style! A lean, mean, oxy-snorting machine! McDonalds didn't have shit on me.

This was the next level after supersizing! Rob had SUPERSIZED me, that's for sure!! My body and mind could devour these narcotics like a supercharged pac-man in the bonus round! Doses that would kill other people barely gave me a buzz. I was falling down the rabbit hole faster and faster and still falling. I didn't know what was at the bottom, but it scared me, and other times, I didn't care! It's scary when you don't care about your well-being as long as you're high going through it.

When I started snorting multiple 160s a day, my life changed. My life was constantly in the ballast! I was riding the razor's edge. A Double-edged blade at that! I can't even count the number of times I woke up choking and gagging with a mouthful of puke. How I never asphyxiated on my puke is, in and of itself, a miracle! I have said this a few times but believe in some higher power. Now I KNOW my higher power allowed me to survive to do precisely what I'm doing. Tell my story and let people know you can survive this, and you will if you want to. That's the bottom line!

I can tell you how I survived, but you must want to stay! It's so easy to give up when you're down that rabbit hole. Just to say fuck it, fuck it all, man! I know I just about did many times, but you must keep fighting. It's essential when you're going through an addiction to always have something to live for, even if it's as mundane as going to visit somewhere you've never been. Mine was always my mother. I thank god every day I survived, not for myself, but for my mother! ALWAYS HAVE SOMETHING TO LIVE FOR and fight daily to survive and get better. It's by far the hardest thing I've ever done or will ever do.

OK, so where were we? So I left Mr Patel's 7-11 and returned to Billy's. Billy was never home and worked all the time! Billy got fucked up a lot but damn sure worked his ass off the next day. Billy was young and strong, though! As soon as I walked into the trailer, the lil monster started his chant of, "Let's snort a pill, Let's snort a pill, let's snort a pill," and the fucker wouldn't stop until I surrendered. The lil monster was very persistent, so I went into the bathroom to snort a pill. It was the same ritual as the" oxy dance." As I raised my head from the glass-top table where I had just snorted the fat ass line the 160 made, I became dizzy. This had never happened before, so it did concern me a bit, but after about 15 seconds, it disappeared and was replaced by a trip to the stars. I fucking loved this shit, and the more I snorted, the more I was curious about what the next level had in store for me. What one more pill would do? Was there a ceiling, or would I keep climbing plateau after plateau in the narcotic heavenly bliss of wonder?

I sat in our recliner in the living room and just blankly stared out the window and the empty acres and acres in front of me. It was a great place to get high, 500 acres of solitude, because no one was ever around except Billy, and he could almost snort as much blow as I could. We made a perfect but scary match as far as roommates go. As I sat there, literally comfortably numb, I remembered Billy had said he had some blow-up in his closet under his jeans. Did I want to do any blow? I asked myself. Would it diminish this great buzz I had in any way, I remembered thinking. "Fuck yeah, let's do a line," the lil monster said! I returned to Billy's bedroom and looked under the jeans in his closet. It was precisely where he said it would be. "What The hell?" I thought! He had some blow, alright! I had only seen a kilo once, and I was sure this was the second time.

Beside the brick was a small baggie with what looked like a couple of grams. I took the small baggie out and went to the kitchen table. Of course, it was a glass top! I laid out a pretty good size line, snorted it in one big swoosh, and sat back down in the recliner. OMG, what a feeling, I remember thinking! Honestly, I couldn't tell if this was a better feeling mixing Coke and oxy, but it was different! I felt great, though. A wave of relief flowed across my body and assured me everything would be alright! As soon as I ran out of the oxys I purchased from Rob, I would quit. Yep, that's exactly what I would do, I thought! I didn't need these pills anymore! I was strong enough to stop! I was a strong motherfucker, and I could do anything my mind set out to do.

Yes, sir, when these were done, so was I! I had done 480 milligrams of oxycodone and a half gram of blow within the last 4 hours. I was 10 feet tall and bulletproof, baby! Who needs pain pills, fuck them! After about 30 minutes, the blow wore off, but so did the oxys. My mind thought the blow had shortened the life and time of the oxy buzz. The lil monster didn't even have to say anything this time. The oxy dance was coming up again. I snorted my 4th 160 of the day, kicked the recliner back as far as it would go, lit a cigarette, and strapped it tight. The second blastoff had begun. I was transitioning back into the Rocketman, ground control to Major Tom; here I come!!

The next thing I remembered after I closed my eyes was Billy waking me up in a panic the following day." Get the fuck up, man, get the fuck up, man, are you alright" he asked? I tried talking, but it came out all gurgling, sounding like I was underwater or something.. I started choking and coughing and realized as I slept I had thrown up all over my chest, legs, and floor. My mouth still had puke in it! There must have been a gallon of this yellowish, sour-smelling shit everywhere. After I cleared my throat where I could speak clearly, I simply said 'Yeah, I'm good; you must have got a lil too fucked up last night". He just shook his head and said, "I'm just glad you're alive." I remember thinking the same thing as I went into the kitchen to get supplies to clean up my mess.

" Gettin' higher baby, gettin' higher baby, gettin' higher baby."

Grand Master Flash

Chapter 31

Keebler Toll House Cookies, Anyone

The next couple of years went by in a flash. I was now averaging about 1000-1600 milligrams of OxyContin in a day. Rob must have had access to tractor-trailers full of these 160s because I was doing tractor-trailer loads, I promise you! The prices all around were going up significantly. People were understanding just how much 160 milligrams of pure oxycodone was worth. It was about this time these pills got the nickname of HILLBILLY HEROIN!

Hell, most of the people I was selling to had never heard of a 160 and thought I was selling them bullshit a lot of times.

When that happened, I would crush up a 160 and tell them to snort as much of it as they wanted. About 5 minutes later, they now were well aware oxy made a 160, a mind-blowing amount of pure oxycodone to do at one time! During this entire time, Rob never charged me more than six bucks a piece. Even down to five bucks a piece if I bought twenty or more! I would buy 200 for a grand, or five bucks each, and then sell 50 for 20 bucks each, pay Rob the grand, and have 150 - 160 mg oxys for FREE! Yes, sir, buddy, I was getting fucked up during this time; I promise you!

I was so far gone and immune to this shit that when I was actually out of pills, the ER visits and mainlining Dilaudid didn't even really get me high. It was more of a last resort to keep me from going through withdrawals. The withdrawals I now faced were the most painful and intense thing you could ever imagine! My body would feel like I was itching from the inside out, and every bone in my body felt broken or was in the process of breaking and on fire! Like there had been a blowtorch inside my body blast burning and torching my bones internally, with a large vice grip tightening and turning inside my stomach!! Anything and everything that had ever happened bad to me in my life would play over and over on this continuous loop in my head! It was every bit of a mental mind fuck and physical torture!

I always called it riding the bull! It was like you being put on the back of a bull, butt naked, and strapped on so you couldn't come off. It lasted until I could find a fix to get off the damn thing! I would do almost anything to avoid getting up on that bull! It was, I was sure, the closest thing to hell you could ever imagine, and it was right here knocking on my front door every morning I awoke! Withdrawing was BRUTAL!! The buzz was not the top priority anymore! It was simply not having to go through starting that now took center stage! I was running with the devil for sure!

Billy came home from work one day and asked me if I wanted to ride with him. "Sure, where are we going?" I asked. "I need to run a lil something over to a buddy of mine. He's cool. His dad owns one of the biggest car dealerships in town. He parties all the time. He also said he had 50- 80 mg oxys and would give me five for making the trip. You can have them if you ride with me." Billy offered. "I'm in," I announced.

As we rode, Billy filled me in more on the character I was getting ready to be introduced to. "He's nuts but cool as hell! He is just one of these guys who doesn't do much because his family is wealthy. He's got a ton of great toys as well. Boats, a helicopter, cars, etc." Billy explained to me. Just as he finished his last sentence, we pulled up into the driveway of a nice ass house in a lovely neighborhood. In the driveway was the baddest airboat I had ever seen! We walked up the brick-lined entrance to the house and found the front door wide open.

"Aaron, hey Aaron, you here? "Billy asked. No response at all. "Is anyone here? "Billy inquired again. "Aaron, it's Billy," he said in a much louder voice. Still no answer. Billy walked into the foyer, and a question popped into my head." Hey man, this dude won't shoot us or anything, will he?" Billy was not worried and calmly said, "No, he's cool."

We walked into this enormous kitchen with a TV blaring the daily news and sports. "Aaron, where the fuck are you? Billy said over and over. No reply at all! We made our way up the spiral staircase. We started walking down a long hall to the main bedroom as Billy continued announcing our presence. We walked into this humongous primary bedroom suite, past the bed, and back to the primary bath.

Billy led the way and started laughing when he turned a corner before me. As I passed the corner, I was amazed at what I saw. There was a guy, I was assuming was Aaron, who had passed entirely out on the toilet! Just like he had casually gone into the restroom to take a shit and had decided in the middle of it to take a nap!

Billy cautiously tapped him on the shoulder, "Hey man, you alright?" and nothing happened. Billy repeated this process, and suddenly, the episode at Byron's came rushing back into my mind. "Is he dead? "I asked. "Fuck, I don't know," Billy responded. "Let's just call 911 on the way out and get out of here," I suggested. Neither of us needs to be caught up in any shit like this," I said. "For sure," Billy answered back. He reached over and repeated what he had attempted the first time. This time, the result was different. Aaron slowly raised his head and said, "Hey Billy, what's going on?".

"UHH, not much. I brought that stuff you wanted, and when we got here, the front door was wide open, and you didn't respond, so we came in ". "I wanted to make sure you were ok," Billy said.

I'm great, brother. Who's this? Aaron looked at me, a bit confused, and asked? "This is my good friend, my roommate I was telling you about, Jimmy. " "Cool, nice to meet you, brother." he raised his hand to shake mine, and yes, he was still sitting on the toilet with his pants down around his ankles! I almost belly laughed but made a joke about it out loud. "Nice to meet you, brother, and what a first impression. I will never forget meeting you, that's for damn sure, "I teased.

We all belly laughed, and Aaron said," You guys go downstairs in the kitchen, and I will be right down" "Make sure you wipe your ass," Billy said, and we all belly laughed again as we made our way downstairs. Billy and I headed back down the spiral staircase into this massive gourmet kitchen. I love to cook, and it was a chef's dream. I had never seen top-of-the-line Viking appliances throughout, with a few wild-looking cooking gadgets!

Billy and I noticed a slight burnt smell but didn't think much of it. If he could fall asleep shitting on the toilet, burning something in the kitchen wasn't too far of a stretch. We laughed! About five minutes later, Aaron came around the corner. He didn't look too bad for a guy that was passed out on the shitter only five minutes ago!

"What's up, my brother?" Aaron said in a very excited voice. Not much, man, just bringing your gift over," Billy announced. "Well, break the shit out then," Aaron said. Billy went down to his sock and then revealed a baggie that, by the looks of it, contained at least a half ounce of coke. Billy handed it to Aaron, and Aaron gave him six crisp, new one-hundred-dollar bills.

"Let's get this party started then," Aaron said, pouring out what looked like at least an eight ball on, you guessed it, another house with an enormous glass-top kitchen table! These types of tables I was learning were prevalent in the greater Ocala area! We all did an extensive ass line and started shooting the shit when Billy asked," Hey man, you got those oxys you were going to give me?". "Yeah, man, I had to hide them in my oven this morning. My sister came over this morning, and she's noisy as hell, so I put them in a place she would never have looked in the oven. I do t think she's ever used one in her life," Aaron said with a mischievous smile. We all laughed as Aaron got up from the table and started walking towards the first two ovens that sat side by side. "OH FUCK!" Aaron yelled out. DAMMIT, MAN!" Aaron said as he opened the oven door and pulled out a cookie sheet that looked like a big, burnt greenish cookie on it. "What the hell is that?" Billy asked. "It's 49-80 milligrams OxyContins," Aaron responded. "I snorted one about two hours ago when I found out my sister was coming. I hid the rest in my second oven, which I never use," Aaron said. "Apparently, you *do* use it," Billy said comically. "Then I got hungry, "Aaron continued, "and came down about an hour ago to preheat the oven to cook my Hungry Man dinner and turned the wrong oven on." We all started laughing so hard I had tears coming out of my eyes.

After Aaron stopped laughing, he said, "Fuck it, still the same drug, just in a lil different form." We all laughed again as Aaron announced, "Would anyone care for an oxy chip-Keebler Toll House cookie? "I would love one, while they're still warm, please, with a big ass cold glass of milk preferably," I laughingly said. "I like this guy," Aaron said, looking at Billy as he started chuckling again. I watched as he broke off a piece of this oxy-cookie-looking thing and placed it on the glass tabletop. "What tha fuck we gonna do with that? "Billy asked. We are gonna grind that shit up and snort it," Aaron said in a very matter-of-factly tone of voice. He proceeded to one of the many cabinets above the Italian marble countertop and pulled out what looked like a coffee grinder. "What's that?" Billy asked. "It's a coffee grinder," Aaron announced. "What in the hell are you gonna do with a coffee grinder? "Billy asked. "Well, I figure I know about how big of a line an 80 mg oxy makes, so we will just grind a bunch up and cut up what looks like an 80 mg oxy line". "Sounds like a plan to me," I concurred. "I guess, hell, I have never done an oxy," Billy said. "What, are you kidding me? Strap it on, brother, you're in for a treat!" Aaron said as he started breaking the cookie up into smaller pieces that would fit in the coffee grinder." No, I'm good," Billy said, 'All I need is one more bad habit," as he laughed, "but every time you guys snort an oxy, I will match you in a line of blow," Billy said laughingly. Aaron ground up 2-3 pieces of oxy he had broken off of this baked monstrosity and ground that shit down to the finest powder I had ever seen, then poured it out on the kitchen table right beside the pile of coke. The only difference after Aaron picked out all the minuscule burnt pieces of oxy was the oxy pile was just not as white. Oxy on the left, blow on the right," Aaron announced, "My new friend, Mr. Powers, you're up. "You guys, by now, know what line I went to first, the oxy pile on the left. I cut out a rather healthy line. Remember, I was used to doing 160 mg lines. "Damn, son, that's a big ass line of oxy there," Aaron said. Oh, I'm sorry, bro; I don't want to seem like a pig," I said. "No, I didn't mean it that way," Aaron said. "Just didn't want you to overdo it," Aaron continued. "Yeah, again, sorry, man, I'm used to crushing up 160s and snorting it all in one big line. Those make a huge ass line," I said laughingly. "WHAT??" Aaron said in a louder voice than we all had been using. "They make oxys in 160 mg pills? "Yes, sir", I said. "OMG, CAN YOU GET ME SOME?" Aaron asked. "Yes sir," I responded, as I did the oxy line in one big swoosh. "How much are they?" he asked. It's according to how many you want," I responded. "Get me a million of them," he laughed out loud. We will talk later." "Sounds good", he said. Man, that fresh line of oxy-baked dust hit me like a ton of bricks. Looking back on it, that line was probably more like 200-240 milligrams cause it propelled me almost instantly backstage with Elton John the Rocketman, damn I felt great. Aaron did an oxy line about half the size of mine, and Billy cut out a line of blow, probably as big as my oxy line. We all sat there like three speeding freight trains just rolling full speed down the track.

We talked about everything from the price of oxys to the price of gold and everything in between. I did a small line of blow and another smaller line of oxy. Aaron followed me snort for snort, and so did Billy, with blow and no oxy. "Man, that's a badass windboat out there," I said. Aaron and Billy started laughing their asses off. "It's a fucking airboat, man," Billy said. "Fuck it, wind boat, airboat, all the same. "Aaron was laughing his ass off and said," Ya know he's right."

"I bet that's a loud ass bitch. What is that, a damn airplane engine in it? "I asked. "Biggest airplane engine you can put in one," Aaron boasted. I looked up, and Billy had cut him another line out, and Aaron said," Cut me and Jimmy an oxy line out too, and then we will go out and fire that bitch up so you can hear it purr! "Cool," Billy responded. He cut out three lines, bent down and snorted the first one, and passed Aaron the bill. Aaron snorted his line, and I finished the ritual. As I snorted the oxy, it tasted exactly like cocaine, but I said nothing. Both of them had gone before me and said nothing. It must just be me, I remember thinking.

Just moments after my revelation, Billy jumped up, ran out the back sliding glass door, bent over, and started throwing up. I ran out and noticed this was another level of fucked up. Billy gets fucked up, but it never goes to where he is falling down and puking everywhere.

"Man, don't know what's wrong," Billy said. Right then, it hit me, and I realized Billy had snorted the wrong line. Billy had snorted 80 milligrams of oxy for the first time in his life. Unknowingly! Aaron ran out, and I brought him up to speed. 'yeah, it makes some folks sick' 'Aaron said. "Yeah, especially doing 80 milligrams or more your first time." 'That's a bunch I said. "What the fuck, will I die?" Billy said. "Not sure," Aaron said as he winked at me. "Possibly," I said, winking back at Aaron. "Nah, man, you just gotta ride it out for a few more minutes' 'I assured him, not really knowing at all, but I didn't want to freak him out anymore than he already was, though! We all sat there for about five more minutes as Billy leveled off. Aaron finally said, "Hey man, let's go fire that windboat up!". We all laughed. Billy finally stood up, and we started slowly but surely, heading out to the front of the house. As we walked out the front door, Billy looked at me and announced, Man, I feel great! This might be the best buzz I've ever had." Oh shit," I silently thought; nothing good can come from that statement, that's for sure! I watched as Aaron climbed over the side of the airboat and jumped up into the driver's seat.

As Aaron sat up high in this probably 4-foot-long seat that was about 5 feet from the bottom of the boat, I looked at Billy to make sure he was still on planet Earth with us! "Hey man, are you doing alright?" I asked!" I'm doing better than alright! This has to be the best buzz I've ever had in my life," Billy announced again. "Yeah, I'm feeling pretty damn good myself," I said. "You know we are all speedballing, just not in the normal fashion," I said. "I don't know what the fuck it's called, but I love it," Billy said again. It gives me chills right now thinking back to this specific space and time because I'm pretty sure if you asked him, Billy would say this was the day he fell in love with pain pills, especially oxys.

Billy went down a hellish path for years, messing with these damn things. To this day, I still feel personally responsible for turning him on to this life-destroying beast, but he survived, thank God! Miraculously, we both did! We are also both Geminis, though. Actually, both were born on June 9th, believe it or not. We were also two very headstrong motherfuckers who somehow, with God's grace, survived! Still, to this day, I have no clue how. Thankfully, we are still close today and can laugh at our war stories together.

Anyway, where were we? Aaron jumped up in that seat and turned the key over to this loud ass whoosh, whoosh, whoosh noise and nothing. He repeated it, and nothing again. "Just forget it, Aaron. It's no big deal," Billy said. "No, I want Jimmy to hear this beast," Aaron replied. He turned it over again, and just when the last whooshing sound came out, and I thought it was just a repeat of the first two attempts, the beast came to life! When I say the beast came to life, it did. It was and still is the loudest damn thing, machine or whatever the hell you wanna call it, I've ever heard in my life!

The spark from the spark plug ignited that airplane fuel, and it combusted in a sound that was mind-blowing. It shot fire three feet long out of the six big ass exhaust pipes and shook the ground I was standing on beside it! It sounded like someone had implanted an airplane engine into your eardrum and brain and gave it full throttle!! Aaron reached down to his side and put on a pair of earphones that had been hanging on the side of the driver's seat. Aaron was laughing like a wild banshee; you couldn't, of course, hear him, but he was smiling ear to ear and had this wild, whacked-out look of a madman, like Dr. Frankenstein smiling and laughing hysterically after he had brought to life some damn monstrosity! I remember thinking, I will never get in that fuckin thing with him, EVER!

Billy was making this motion with his arms, both going up and down like the way quarterbacks do in football games to quiet the crowd down. Just as I turned back to look at Aaron, he grabbed this big stick and handle-looking contraption, pulled it back towards him, and did something with his foot. I've since learned it was the actual throttle that controls the damn thing! When he did this, all hell broke loose! This damn thing started screaming in this loud ass, deep, thundering, Earth-shattering noise, and suddenly, it leaped off the front of the trailer and set loose! It was like we had turned a damn bull loose and were heading to gut the matador! "Was this thing gonna fucking fly?" I remember thinking! Does it double as a damn plane too? I remember my high mind thinking. Was he just gonna peace us out, take off, cruise around the county for a few minutes, and bring this damn thing back for a landing in his cul-de-sac like a redneck flying saucer?

I remember being so high and confused, like, WTF! When I noticed Billy's face, I was in literal shock! I remember thinking, he's probably thinking the same shit I am, WTF IS GOING ON! As It leaped forward, it flew off of the trailer and shot down the street about 50 feet as sparks and shit flew off of the bottom of the boat. My mind now knew and realized, WOW, he had fucked up his boat. We both ran up beside him as he turned the beast off, and it came to a now deafening silence. Billy was just sitting there with his mouth wide open, not having or knowing anything to say. I just said, "That's a bad bitch," and we all started laughing again.

"Fuck it. I will get it all fixed up. I forgot I released the trailer strap earlier this morning when I was cleaning it," Aaron said as we casually walked back up the driveway to the house. "Do you need us to help you do anything?" Billy asked. "No, I'm good, "Aaron responded. Wonder what Triple A will think about this call?" Aaron said as we all started laughing our asses off again. "We gotta roll, Aaron," Billy continued. I said, "Nice to meet you, Aaron; thanks for the hospitality." He said, "Cool, you as well! Oh, by the way, Jimmy, Billy can give you my number. Call me. Remember, I need a million 160s". We all laughed again as Billy started the truck, and we eased down the road!

"If you lose hope, somehow you lose the vitality that keeps you moving,

You lose that courage to be, That quality that helps you go on in spite of it all.

And so today, I still have a dream."

Dr. Martin Luther King

Chapter 32

Pharmacy Happy Hour

The next couple of years seemed to fly by. I continued my

purchase of the 160s. 160s at five bucks a piece and sold them for twenty to twenty-five. This made it where all of mine were free. An addict's dream becomes actual "FREE PILLS." Not just any free pills, though, 160 mg OxyContin! The strongest narcotic ever produced, or ever has been created in pill form. Honestly, thinking back now, I don't even remember getting high during this time. There were a few instances when I did a half pill more or something and felt that brief rush. However, so briefly, it was all about not getting sick; that's all it had become about anymore.

I barely remember those good ole days when I regularly blasted off into space. Not having to load the chute and get on that bull! That's what my daily goal was now. I was no longer meeting Elton and the Rocket Man much; instead, I was just trying to keep from being deathly ill and opening up on Rodeo night!

If you have never been through this awful cycle, it is hard to explain. Let's just put it this way: death seems like a viable option, trust me! Anyway, again, the next couple of years were a blur. I had moved into a small rental house by myself and was doing the same thing every day. Get up and snort 160-240 milligrams of oxycodone

(I had even tried snorting two 160s at a time). A couple of times, I didn't get any higher, making me sick to my stomach.

My routine became a pill or pill and a half every morning. I was so bad I would crush them up and lay the line on my nightstand before bed. Every morning, I would wake up feeling like death, roll over, snort the line of oxy, and lay back down for fifteen minutes. Then I would get up feeling just fine! Many mornings, though (they were becoming increasingly frequent now), I would wake up with a bed and mouth full of puke. I would choke and spit it out and roll over and snort the line while lying and swimming in my vomit.

Fifteen minutes later, I would roll back over, get up, and clean it all up like nothing ever happened! Then go see Rob, pick up more pills, deliver more pills, and, of course, snort more pills! The end of the day would involve me sitting on the edge of my bed, wondering and sometimes crying in vain and wondering how much longer I had to live, how much longer my body, mind, and soul could continue living in this hell I had created! Then again, I would wake up, snort a pill immediately so I wouldn't be sick, and do the same thing, OVER AND OVER AND OVER, like a fucking rat in the same maze daily with no way out!!

Billy had called me one afternoon, just before I was getting ready for my daily pity party session, and said he was going to this local bar we used to go to and sing karaoke for happy hour. Billy asked me if I wanted to join him. I had just snorted a 160 and said I would meet him. I walked into the bar and sat beside Billy on a bar stool. "What's been going on, man," Billy asked. "Not much brother, same old, same old," I responded.

About this time, an older gentleman walked up to the empty barstool beside Billy and said, "How are you doing, son"? I remember thinking, who in the hell is this guy? I knew it wasn't Billy's dad because I had often met him." Not much, Mike, how have you been? "Pretty good. Can't complain," he said. "Oh, this is Jimmy, one of my good friends," Billy said as he introduced me. "This is Mike, Jimmy. He owns the pharmacy on Oak Street". "HE OWNS WHAT????" the lil' monster screamed in my head! I hadn't had many conversations with the lil monster lately. He has been fed very well recently! I couldn't hardly speak. My high opioid mind was spinning like the fastest toy top ever made, trying to figure out how to make this guy my new best friend!

"Very nice to meet you, Mike," I said. "You as well, Jimmy," Mike said. "You two take care of yourself and stay out of trouble," he said as he stood up and walked back over to the person he spoke to before coming over to visit us. "He's cool, loves to drink, though," Billy said. "Comes here every day for happy hour." "DING, DING, DING the lil monster chirped in. "Guess we know where our new hangout will be," came to mind as they laughed hysterically inside my head! I tried not to be too obvious, but I started mysteriously running into Mike almost daily at a happy hour for the next few months.

The lil monster had given me a specific game plan on approaching this very fragile subject of getting this pharmacy owner to offer or sell us pills! I had mentioned nothing about pills purposely for the first couple of months. Unless he brought it up, I decided I wouldn't! One afternoon, I walked into the bar, and the little monster said, "This is getting old. We must find out soon if he will play ball with us, and I agree. The next time he was three-quarters drunk, which more than likely would be today, I would casually mention it.

Mike walked in as expected. I drank my Mr Pibb, and Mike drank his crown as usual. A couple of hours later, I noticed he began his normal slurring of words. The little monster picked up on it immediately and screamed, "Today is the day, Jimmy," of course, as always, I agreed with him! "How's business been lately?" I asked. This was a typical question I had asked many times in the last couple of months to make sure when I asked this question when I was ready to ask him about pills; it would just seem like a normal old conversation we always had.

"Business has been very good. I have been getting a larger than normal amount of pain pills to refill, though," he said. "YIPPIE! "the little monster screamed. "Let's walk right through that door he just opened, Jimmy." I laughed on the inside. The lil monster was a funny lil fucker sometimes, I thought. "Hmmm, wonder why? "I asked. "No idea," he said, but the money's good. Again, the little monster yelled at the top of his voice," And he likes money, Jimmy; it's time to take our prey down, or at least take the shot," again, as you guys probably already know, I agreed with him! "Yeah, I hear ya," I said." People love 'em.' I could sell a 55-gallon drum of them if I had them and laughed immediately after I said it to make it sound like I was joking".

"Well, what time would you like to pick up your 55-gallon drum tomorrow, Jimmy"? Mike asked." WTF did he just say?" the lil monster asked. I asked myself the same question and wondered if I had heard him say what I thought he did. I just blurted out. "How's noon sound? "I said again, laughing. "Seriously, would you like to buy some? He asked the magic question, and best of all, the slurring of words had stopped, and he was as serious as a heart attack. Yes, I'm dead serious. I want to buy some," I said. "What kind do you want?" Mike said in a lower, more serious tone of voice. "160 mg OxyContin," I replied. "Damn, you know exactly what you want, huh?" Mike asked. "Yes sir, I do," I responded. "I don't keep any of those in stock. It's the most powerful narcotic pill on the market, and the feds are keeping close tabs on the number of 160s and where they are going. "I can, however, get you the 80s if you want them," Mike stated. "Yeah, those would be just fine," I responded.

To make a long story short, I started purchasing the 80s from Mike. This supply, along with Rob's 160s, made for a marriage in heaven for an opioid attack like me until one day it didn't! It was the strangest thing, and I now think about the sequence of events, and there had to be divine intervention. Just out of the blue one day, Rob called and said, "I'm out, Jimmy." "What the fuck you mean you're out" the lil monster screamed, as I calmly asked," Forever"? "Yes, forever," Rob calmly said.

"It's been a pleasure getting to know you over these last few years, and I will likely see you around somewhere," he continued. "My pleasure as well, Rob, take care. " That was as short and sweet as it was! I had just lost my unlimited supply of 160s for five bucks each. WTF! I bet you I had purchased over 100,000 - 160s in the last two to three years without incident. He was always where he said to meet. He always had the 160s and stayed true to his word on price and quantity. This was extremely rare in the drug trade world, and I knew it!

They had killed the golden goose, and I knew there would never be another Rob, and there wasn't! It didn't slow me down much, though, at the beginning. The main thing was that the profit I was making from buying the 160s from Rob and reselling them gave me my 160s for free, NOT ANYMORE! The 80s cost me twice what a 160 had been, and I could only resale them for half the price I was reselling the 160s for. It's not too hard to do the math. I noticed I was almost always out of pills and cash. I knew in my gut I didn't have long left.

Mike told me one day at the bar the DEA was coming down very hard on opioids and especially oxys. He just couldn't get away with selling me anymore. Looking back, I just calmly said, "ok," when the lil monster was having a full-blown panic attack inside of me and was continually screaming, "WHAT IN THE FUCK ARE WE GONNA DO JIMMY?" and For once, I didn't have an answer for him. I talked Mike into selling me the last 100 - 80s and told myself I wouldn't sell or do anymore when they were gone; I would simply ride the bull and quit. The same lie I had told myself over a million times in the last ten years.

This time, I was going to, though, I thought in my mind, and of course, I was high as hell when deciding this action. D-day finally arrived one day when I woke up covered in my puke and feeling like a train had just run over me. I only had 3 - the 80s left, so I rolled over, snorted one, got up, put my clothes on, and went for a ride. I rode around in vain, thinking about how I had destroyed my life and wondering just how to survive and live a life without opioids. I honestly couldn't see or imagine what that looked like. Gone were the days of snorting pills and feeling great and not worrying about a damn thing. Those days were far in the rear-view mirror.

The only thing snorting pills did now was keep me from getting sick. That's it! I drove back home, snorted another pill, and tried to stay positive, but it was not possible. I snorted the last 80 at about 6 o'clock. I sat just rewinding 10+ years over and over in my head and just asking myself why. I finally fell asleep at about midnight. You guys will think I'm making this up, but just like this entire book, it's 100% true, as I remember.

After I fell asleep, I drifted off into my typical airplane dream again. I hadn't had it for a while. The plane was screeching and breaking apart as it was heading down towards the ground, and just as it was about to hit the ground, instead of flashing forward to the hangar with caskets and body parts, I woke up. I woke up choking and gagging and trying to breathe, and I couldn't! I lodged something in my throat; it felt like, and even after all the puke was out of my mouth, I still couldn't breathe. I ran into my bathroom, and when I looked in the mirror, I swear I saw myself as a dead person whose face had survived an airplane crash but whose life did not. My face looked like it had torn gashes in it. Half of my skull on the top left of my head was just missing! The scariest thing I can see as clear as day as I'm writing this was my smile, one of those long-ass-mouth horror smiles that goes from one ear to the other. The one eyeball, with the tendons and everything hanging down, was lying in the left corner of that mouth.

After seeing this, I bent down and stuck my finger probably down to my navel and started throwing up. At first, I threw up an enormous chunk of something that looked like a peach pit. After that came out, I could breathe and continued throwing up the usual ultraviolet yellowish, greenish, acidic sour-tasting shit like I always did when I was withdrawing. I finally stopped throwing up and washed my face and hands off. I sat on the end of the bed that was afloat with what looked like gallons of sour-smelling puke and just

cried like a baby.

"It is better to travel on the rough right road than smooth, wrong way."

Lailah Gifty Akita

Chapter 33

Just Do It

After what must have been an hour, the little monster started wailing and yelled at me to "GET UP, quit blubbering like a baby, and get to the ER!" Without thinking twice, I sprang out of bed, took my car keys, and drove to the nearest hospital. Fortunately, it was the one I had visited the least so far. When I arrived, I entered the lobby by doing my best 'Kidney Stone Academy Award dance.' As expected, they immediately wheeled me back into a chair to a bed. The little monster began doing his joyous jig and singing, "I get high with a little help from my friends." I remember slightly chuckling as this was all new to me.

Suddenly, the privacy drapes pulled back, and I heard, "Mr. Powers, my name is Dr. Howe," he said, hesitantly introducing himself. His sudden appearance obviously puzzled me before the actual treatment had begun. My mind raced as I tried to make sense of the situation, but only one thought came to mind: let's get this over with and move on to the next thing. As he spoke, I couldn't help but think that something wasn't right, that there was more going on than just my invisible kidney stones. "Mr. Powers, do you need help?" Dr. Howe asked me with concern in his voice. What kind of question is that? Of course, I need help!

I was here for a reason! My thoughts turned sour, and my mood darkened as I realized what he was insinuating. "You've been here five times in the past three years for kidney stones, which isn't normal," Dr. Howe continued. "Do you have a problem with opioids? Are you addicted to them?" I wanted to scream at him, to tell him I needed the drugs because of how much pain I was in every time I came here and that if they would take care of my stones properly, maybe I wouldn't be so reliant on them! But all that came out was an icy stare.

Staring at him without a word, I got up and ripped off the admission bracelet they had put on me moments before. I dashed out of the emergency room entrance, crying hysterically as I drove home. All my wrongdoings ran through my mind on constant repeat. When I entered my house, I collapsed onto the couch and wept. My body shook uncontrollably due to pain and fear of how sick I already was and what was going to come next. Desperately, I searched for something to help me get through it one last time. An hour later, it turned dark outside, and so did my mind. Feeling like the walls were shrinking around me, I realized there wasn't a backup plan or strategy this time; all else hadn't failed for a long time, but now I couldn't think straight.

My mind was in overdrive, and I couldn't make sense of my thoughts. Desperate, I stumbled towards the kitchen to get a glass of water. But it only made things worse. The taste of sour bile mixed with blood was now present when I spat in the sink, sending my heart racing like never before. Hopelessly, I cried out to God that I was tired of suffering and wanted Him to take me home. Just then, a little voice interrupted: "Get your crying, blubbering ass off the couch, grab your car keys, and follow me. I have an idea!"

I started the car and drove to where the little monster's plan would come to fruition. I parked in the back of the lot, near some trees. When I opened the trunk, I grabbed the object the little monster had told me to get from my house before we left on this mission impossible-style undertaking. As I stood behind the pharmacy, soaked in my putrid, acidic, sour sweat from going through withdrawals for six hours, something wet and sticky ran across my fingers that clutched a 40-pound concrete block. That's when I noticed a one-inch gash in my forefinger dripping red blood onto my feet and onto the asphalt. Was I really about to toss this enormous block of cement into the front plate-glass window of my friend's pharmacy and steal as many opiates as possible, then make off with my goodies? Was I the Grinch or Santa Claus? Why in the hell did I ask myself that question anyway! My mind felt like it was in a massive tornado of shit! Nothing made sense anymore.

Have all the years I've lived led up to this one exchange? What thoughts got me so close to a decision that could land me in jail for a decade? "Fuck it," my opiate-deprived brain protested, and its devilish companion agreed. I stepped out of the foliage, hauling a cinder block with me as the dark red liquid seeped from various spots. In complete darkness, I stumbled onward until I reached the pharmacy's giant plate-glass window that said "PHARMACY." The little monster inside my head demanded action, and my drug-starved brain didn't hesitate to comply. "FUCK IT," was my last thought as I hoisted the concrete block over my head. No sooner had I begun swinging it over my head, some invisible force pushed down from behind and knocked it out of my hand; if not for it, the cinder block would have crashed through the plate-glass window.

I saw headlights coming down the hill toward the pharmacy, and I threw myself on the ground, praying that whoever drove by wouldn't notice me. Tears filled my eyes as a wave of panic and pain crashed over me. My stomach was in knots, and it felt like I couldn't move; fear had rendered me paralyzed. I lay there for what seemed like ages but was merely a few minutes. Eventually, I mustered up the energy to return to my car and drive home. When I arrived at my house, I collapsed on the floor and screamed out to God. "God, if you're real and care about me, please help me! Take away the pain and free me from this addiction. I can't keep living like this! Please help me!" The phrase "Please help me" repeated repeatedly until finally fading into silence.

The longest journey starts with the first step, but that step has to be

forward and not backward."

James Powers

Chapter 34

Methadonia Madness

When I opened my eyes, I was still on the floor, in the same spot where I had begged God for help the night before. My vision and head were foggy from a mixture of sweat and vomit. It felt like someone had taken a sledgehammer to my skull. In horror, I recalled every detail of the previous night. I'm not sure if this sounds strange, but I firmly believe my late cousin Johnny's spirit stopped me from throwing that concrete block; just as I was raising the block to throw it, something pushed down onto it with extraordinary strength and knocked it out of my hands. His presence lingered afterward, and even though he's in heaven and we haven't talked about it yet, I know in my heart it was him. When I woke up, I felt terrible both mentally and physically. Suddenly, an idea came into my mind--someone told me methadone could be obtained at clinics for 12 dollars a day. Without delay, I looked up the number in the phone book and called them.

"I've developed an addiction to pain pills, and I'm suffering from withdrawals; please help," I said to the woman on the phone. "When was the last time you took opioids?" she inquired. I replied that it had been about 48 hours since my last dose, although some exaggeration was involved in that statement. "If you can make it here by 1pm, we can begin paperwork while you get bloodwork done and then proceed with treatment if applicable," she told me. "What do you need blood work for?" I asked. "You must first do the bloodwork to see the doctor; if all is okay, he'll give you a dose of methadone that should start working within 15-20 minutes," the woman explained. "That's great," I said. Then came one more question: how much will this cost me? She answered that the first visit would be 262 dollars for the blood work and doctor's visit, plus $12 per day for each dose of methadone afterward. The woman explained that I only needed to take one dose a day. After my initial 262 dollar payment, the daily cost was only 12 bucks. "So once I pay the first sum, it's just twelve bucks daily," I asked? "Yes, that is correct," she replied.

I glanced at the clock- it was 12:40, so I had twenty minutes to get there. Before calling the place, I'd looked up the address and knew it would take me 15-20 minutes of driving. "Okay, thanks," I said, "I'm on my way." The woman reminded me to bring my ID and not be late--"1 pm sharp, we lock the door," she warned. "Oh, I won't," I responded before hanging up the phone and finding my flip-flops. Then, I drove as fast and safely as possible toward the methadone clinic. When I finally arrived, it was 12:50--so I had made it in plenty of time. The clinic itself was situated in a seedy strip mall-like area. There must have been 40-50 people lined up outside; they all appeared worse off than myself, and I felt like I had just pulled up for an open audition for The Walking Dead.

As I pulled into the parking lot of the methadone clinic, I noticed many familiar faces from my days living in Lexington and visiting the thriller video production once. I couldn't help but laugh as I saw open drug deals taking place right there in the parking lot. It seemed like a great place to sell any opioid; you had people who were sure to need and want what you had! As soon as I stepped out of the car, thriller guy number 1 asked me if I needed anything. It was such an obvious question - I almost looked as bad as he did! Of course, I needed something! Instead, I answered, "Nah, I'm good." I also proceeded to get in line with what looked like at least 40 other folks in dire need. At 12:55, I knew I wouldn't make it by 1 o'clock, so I asked the skinny dude next to me, "Hey man, what happens at one?". "They lock the door, and anyone that doesn't get in goes over there and gets what they need from the guy in the black car," he snickered. Out of nowhere, the little monster in my head shouted louder than I'd ever heard, "Just use the 262 bucks in your pocket and buy whatever you can from the black car, and let's get out of here!" That sounded like a good plan. Still, something seemed off - for once I had more willpower than him. So, I returned to my conversation with the skinny dude and said: "I was told to be here before 1 to do bloodwork and get my first dose." He inquired if it was my initial dose, to which I responded it was. He then told me that a door for new intake patients was down the other end of the corridor. Grateful for the information, I began walking towards the entrance, where no soul was waiting in line.

The stench of rot and despair was overwhelming as I passed through the queue. It reminded me vividly of how bad things were when I was coming down off my high. I had to suppress a gag reflex; it was so intense! Then, at precisely 12:59, the door flew open, and this big dude bellowed, "Two more! That's it!" Suddenly, like ants marching towards a picnic blanket laden with food, the line scattered towards the parking lot. It seemed comical but was actually quite saddening. I had already guessed that both the proprietors of this place and the police were aware of what was going on but didn't care much. I reached for the second door handle, and it suddenly opened, revealing an even bigger and meaner-looking guy who asked gruffly if I was there for intake? "No motherfucker, I'm here to buy a new car," the little monster screamed inside my head. I smiled brightly and answered, "Yes, sir, I am." Unimpressed, he grabbed my arm firmly and pulled me inside before slamming the door shut. "Place it over there," he instructed in a stern voice. "Okay," I replied sheepishly. This guy reminded me of one of those young guys trying to make it in the WWF. I could tell he was completely jacked up on steroids and probably wanted to be there even less than I did. He walked over to the window and mumbled something before an older woman, probably in her mid-to-late sixties, emerged behind a door and introduced herself. "What's your name, young man?" she asked kindly. "My name is James Powers," I responded. "When was the last time you took any opioids?" she asked. "About 48 hours ago," I answered honestly. "Okay, follow me, please." "Yes, ma'am." We walked through the door and into a room that had been set up for drawing blood. Looking back on it now, it looked like some dingy old back room where you'd go to a low-budget used car lot to sign the final paperwork for your 35% loan! Everything felt extraordinarily unsanitary and plain dirty since I arrived here 15 minutes ago. Still, I would roll in shit to feel better at this point.

"My name is Nurse Jones, and I'll be taking your blood sample. Are you allergic to any medications?" she asked me. "No, ma'am," I replied. She then told me to place my left arm in a sling apparatus, which presented it like a bullseye in the middle of my arm, before she inserted the needle into the large vein there. After a few questions, typical for any nurse, she put a bandage on my vein and said I could go back out front and wait for the doctor, who would be with me in 15 minutes. As I sat there waiting, a single tear ran down my cheek as reality sunk in that this was what my life had become, seated in a dirty-ass methadone clinic in Bumfuck Ocala, Florida. About fifteen minutes later, I heard the lock of the outer door open, and that big ass WWF wanna-be leaped up in an instant to greet whoever was coming through the door. I wouldn't want to be that person, I thought.

"Howdy Doc," he said as a skeletal figure in jeans and cowboy boots stepped through the door. "You must be James?" He asked me. I nodded and followed him to a cramped room that reeked of old cigarettes. Sitting behind an unsteady card table, he asked, "So you're addicted to opioids, right?" Before he could ask anything else,

I said, "It's been 48 hours since my last dose." My response made him laugh. "You a mind reader, too? You got my question all ready!" he exclaimed. With a deep chuckle, he coughed and reached for his Marlboro reds, lighting one while holding it in his 6 nicotine-stained front teeth. "Well, I'm a be prescribing you a methadone program. How many opiates have you been using per day? And what kind?" He was inquiring intently. "On average these past couple of years, it's been about 1,200-1,600 milligrams of oxycodone a day—I'd snort 8-10, 160mg oxys a day," I replied with complete honesty. His expression of shock still lingers in my memory today. "Holy shit! Ten 160s a day?!" "Yeah, on average," I said. "Damn, that's a shit ton of opiates! You might be the record holder here!" I was shocked to see a man like this even phased. I decided to lighten the mood, so I said jokingly, "That's quite the record to have—should we call Guinness?" My joke didn't amuse the doctor as much as I thought it would. "Let's try and look on the bright side—at least you're alive!" The doctor said, "How long have you been taking that many?" To which I answered, "For a few years now." He then said something that I'll never forget. "Mr Powers, you should have been dead about a year or two ago. Incredibly, we're here together right now. You're so fortunate to be alive!" When I heard that, all the color drained from my face. All I could say in response was, "I know, doc!"

"Alright," he said. "I'm going to prescribe you 60mg of methadone. Take it today and return tomorrow at 1 pm to see your progress." "That's it?" I asked. "Yep, that's it," he responded. "Will the withdrawal symptoms go away?" I questioned with hope. "You should definitely feel better, and the withdrawal symptoms should subside," he said matter-of-factly. I thought, 'Subside?' What does that even mean? I want them gone! I couldn't think of anything else to say, so I replied with a 'Thanks.' "You're welcome," he said as he lit up his second or third cigarette, polluting the room further with smoke. "The nurse will have your dose ready at the window when you leave. Good luck, and see you tomorrow." As I got up, the worst abdominal pain I'd ever felt hit me like a ton of bricks; the fireman meant serious business. Before exiting, I asked one last question: "Hey Doc, where is the restroom?" He pointed to the first door on the left, then added, "Make sure there is toilet paper in there!" He let out a small laugh before continuing, "Oh, BTW, those shits should go away in 15 minutes too." His yellow teeth gleamed through a jack-o'-lantern-type smile and seemed to show me how to use the restroom.

I went to the front desk after using the restroom, and the lady handed me a cup with sixty milligrams of methadone inside. "Drink all of it," she said, "and you should feel better by tomorrow when you come back. If we need to increase your dosage, we will." At this, the little monster said, "We need more for sure!" I downed the solution—with its reddish-pink hue—before walking out the door. The wrestling, transformer-looking dude standing guard grunted at me as I exited. When I opened the door, it was as if I had stepped into a ghost town: not another soul in sight in the strip center or parking lot. Although I could write an entire book about my experience with methadone, for brevity's sake, I'll condense it here. The next day, after the medication had taken away my withdrawal symptoms, I returned and pretended that I needed a higher dosage.

I explained that I still felt awful, and the next day, they gave me 80 milligrams of methadone. They said they would increase my dosage by 20 milligrams each day if I kept to my story of not getting any better. The little monster inside me kept pushing me to get more and more medicine. It was the same every day until I reached 160 milligrams—the maximum amount the clinic would give anyone. It certainly ended the withdrawal symptoms, but it also got me so messed up that one day, I actually fell asleep while driving through a school zone at five miles per hour! All I remember is waking up with some angry helicopter mom screaming at my window. "I'm sorry, ma'am," I stammered. "I worked all night and thought I'd rest my eyes when I saw the school zone sign and stopped at the stop sign. I didn't realize you were in front of me." Thankfully, I was moving so slowly that my car didn't scratch hers. "Just make sure you get some sleep before you drive again," she said sternly. "Yes, ma'am," I replied before quickly leaving the scene. By this point, I was taking 160 milligrams of liquid methadone daily.

This stuff was even worse than the oxycodone, but you never got that euphoric high. I still felt better after taking it, but I had to go to that damn clinic every day and hand over twelve dollars before I could get my dosage. Then, one of the guys in the parking lot got shot! The whole place was so shady and gave me this feeling of dread. It made me physically feel better, but mentally, things just kept getting worse. I was as broken as a person could be: jobless and scraping together whatever money I could to get hold of enough cash to "dose," as they called it.

Fortunately, I found employment with a new insurance company; I'd be up early each morning to get my dose of methadone before heading off to work. It was intense, as just one small cup kept me going during my twelve-hour shifts. I met a colleague who worked out constantly, and we became friends. Joining him in his exercise regime had given me newfound energy, so much so that I reduced my methadone dose. However, anything less than 80 mgs didn't seem to agree. I decided to go cold turkey but failed miserably; as it turns out, if you stop visiting the methadone clinic regularly, they kick you out. After two days of no sleep due to withdrawal symptoms, I returned, only to be turned away. I was outraged!

I told my boss I was sick and couldn't work. As a result, the next month of my life became a living nightmare. I barely had any sleep for 30 days. To keep my job, I'd take sleeping pills at night, which would only last until the very next day. Thankfully, I would find a pill here and there just so I could continue working. It was the most miserable experience of my life, and it terrified me. All I craved was a sense of normality again, but I couldn't shake this feeling that maybe, just maybe, I would never feel normal. This thought kept running through my mind like an endless loop.

Additionally, I started having stomach pains all the time. I became so constipated that one morning, it felt like my gut was going to explode, and I couldn't move, not even an inch! After some effort, I managed to crawl to the bathroom in search of relief, but nothing happened after trying so hard to push something out.

I was so desperate that I filled a 2-liter bottle with water and attempted to give myself an enema. Don't ever try this--it hurts like hell! Physically and mentally, I just felt like I could not go on. One day, after finally falling asleep on my couch, I awoke with the worst pain in my neck that I had ever experienced; it was so excruciating that it brought tears to my eyes. Worried that I had broken my neck in some crazy way in my sleep, I called 911 and was rushed to the hospital, where I had already been six times for kidney stones. They didn't do anything for me except give me a prescription for 10 Lortab pills and the number of a spinal doctor. I left, got the pills filled, took them all at once, and then called the spinal doctor, who gave me an emergency appointment for the next day. After some x-rays and an MRI, he wrote me a prescription for 60 - 10mg Percocet pills; these were my magic medication--my solid rocket booster fuel—Oxycodone! My logical mind quickly did the math and figured out that the entire bottle would be equivalent to less than 4-160s of Oxy. I rushed to Walgreens near my house to drop off the prescription, then went home in a daze. As I sat on my couch and sobbed like an infant, I knew that these sixty Percocets would last me two, maybe three days at most. I was confident that I'd take ten pills at a time and probably three times each day. That would only delay the inevitable: when I ran out, withdrawal symptoms would start, and I'd be back at square one. I had heard about a new drug for addicts like me called Suboxone. Still, I dismissed it as being similar to methadone--just another way to unsuccessfully chase the dragon.

My body was suddenly engulfed in an uncontrollable trembling and shaking. I rolled off the couch, where I had been lying, and started to cry until I hyperventilated. With my last breath, I screamed out a plea: "God, please help me! I can't take this life anymore. If you're real and listening, save me from this pain!" All I could do was lie there, bawling and thinking about my addiction. The monster within me needed to be fed, but food was not the answer. After managing to calm myself down slightly, I realized that nothing else had worked for me so far, including the methadone clinics, which take advantage of sick people without offering any actual cure. Suppose anyone is even slightly contemplating taking a trip down the methadone rabbit hole. In that case, I implore them to avoid it at all costs, as it only brings temporary relief.

I'd tried many things before, but nothing worked. I got out my iPhone and searched for Suboxone doctors. I was about to hit "close" on the search and go get the Percocet instead when an unseen force changed my mind and convinced me to look further into it. I can't explain why; it was almost a compulsion. Thank goodness that I followed this inner urging—who knows what would have happened if I hadn't? It was the first in a long series of steps that would wind up saving my life. Even though so many pieces needed to fit together to fully rebuild my life, you can't complete a puzzle without the first piece. This decision was the first piece in the puzzle to put James Marion Powers II back together!.

" On your darkest days do not try to see the end of the tunnel by looking far ahead. Focus only on where you are right now. Then carefully take one step at a time, by placing just one foot in front of the other. Before you know it, you will turn that corner "

Anthon St. Maarten

Chapter 35

Along Comes Superman

As I sat there struggling to cope with my mental health, the only thing I could think of to do was search online for a new drug that I had heard of called Suboxone. Although I was not tech-savvy, I even knew how to use Google, so that's what I did. It showed me a few different doctors, and, for some inexplicable reason, I went with

Dr. William Leach because of a higher power than myself. What drew me to him was that it said he was both a family doctor and an addiction specialist who could be accessible 24/7. That statement shouted out to me he must genuinely care about his patients.

PLEASE CALL US OR TEXT US FOR AN IMMEDIATE RESPONSE.

DR LEACH WILL BE SPEAKING WITH YOU PERSONALLY.

CALL -555-1212

I was too scared to pick up the phone and dial the number, so I texted instead. It wasn't long before my phone started ringing. It was a number I didn't recognize, but on impulse, I answered it. "Is this James?" the voice asked. "Yes, sir," I replied. 'James, this is Dr Leach. I understand how hard it must have been for you to make this call, but he said I'm here to help you, not judge you. Those words blew me away for years. I had been searching for someone to understand my situation and explain why my life had become such a mess. He asked me to tell him everything from the start, and when I joked he might not have enough time to hear it all, he told me he did.

"Let me help you," Dr. Leach said. I remember wondering if I was dreaming? I asked, "How much is this going to cost me?" How could this stranger possibly care about my situation? He responded with something that shook me: "I've been a doctor since the late 70s and have taken an oath to help people, not for money but to make a difference. As an addiction specialist, I want to help people like you understand you have a disease, not an evil character. We can manage it with treatment and dedication from both of us, and you can return to your normal self again." Tears started streaming down my face as I tried to compose myself. He didn't utter a word in the next 2-3 minutes as I continued sobbing. I had searched for a person like Dr. William Leach for nearly 15 years, and now I believed my higher power led me right to him while I still had a chance at life! After I stopped crying, all he said was, "Let's start from the beginning: How did you become addicted to opioids?" I followed his instructions and recounted everything I could remember from the beginning until I texted his phone number. For over an hour, he listened without interrupting me. When we finished the call, which lasted 83 minutes, I was shocked and had to check how long we were on the phone. When I joked, "Okay, the end," he replied, "I know this will be one of the most challenging things you'll ever do, James. But don't pick up that prescription of Percocets. Can you do that?" "Okay, doc," I agreed. "But I'm going to feel Like shit tomorrow morning." "Yes," he acknowledged, "you're going to feel terrible in the morning."

"Can you make it to my office by 9am?" he asked. "If you can, I promise that by noon, you'll feel better than you do now. All it will take is trust in yourself first, and then me. I'll give you the roadmap, but you'll have to drive it and follow every instruction - not just for a few days, but for the rest of your life." I considered his words. It was a lot to ask, but something about his earnest manner made me believe in him. "You've got my word," I replied. "I'll be there at 9am."

I arrived early to see Dr. William Leach at nine am the following day. By noon, after my first Suboxone dose, I was feeling much better. I will never forget one statement in particular he made. He asked me if I remembered the first day I took a pain pill for the first time? "It's etched in stone, doc," I assured him. Well, please forget that day; erase it entirely from your brain. Those days of misery and that vicious cycle are over. Always remember today, though. Today is the first day of an arduous journey to regain your life. He had given me the gift of life back. The thing that amazed me and still amazes me is he educated me over the years about my disease. He took the time to sit me down and explain why I was like this. Try having your local methadone clinic do that! He explained everything from A to Z and took his precious time to learn who I was and what made me tick. He's the most humble human being I have ever met or probably ever will! It's simple: HE CARES! He runs a simple program. Do exactly what he says, and he will save your life. Amen! And so it has been; my life has never been better than it is now. For this, there isn't any way to thank someone for saving my life. Dr. William Leach gave me a second chance; I don't know how to express my eternal gratitude.

Thank you so very much, Dr William Leach; if not for your caring and taking 83 minutes out of your day to care enough for someone you didn't even know, I'm sure I would have been just another lost statistic in the opioid epidemic! AGAIN, I DON'T KNOW HOW TO EVEN START TO THANK SOMEONE FOR SAVING MY LIFE; YOU SAVED MY LIFE, AND FOR THIS, I WILL BE ETERNALLY GRATEFUL TO YOU!

Epilogue

Why? Most importantly, why not?!

As I come to the end of this book, I have mixed emotions. I want to thank my wife again. She is my rock! She edited this book and learned things I'm sure she didn't know about my past and I'm sure some did not sit very well with her, but we talked going into this project and I forewarned her of things to come and told her she didn't have to do it, but she genuinely wanted to help me with it and I so appreciate her patience, understanding, and love for me. She, (until the first person reads this) is the first to know my true story from beginning to end. God bless you, my angel, I LOVE AND ADORE YOU! I'm now 60 years old and have to live with the fact that 1/4 of my life I wasted on opioids. I destroyed relationships I could never have back. Did things I'm very ashamed of as a man, and a human being. Writing this book has been very therapeutic. This is the first time my story has been told out loud from beginning to end! It's sort of like burying an old friend.

An old friend you love to hate, if you know what I'm talking about. I buried that little bastard years and years ago! The lil 'monster burned at the stake! I still believe (as my mother instilled in me) that everything happens for a reason. That I have choreographed every step in my life so far to get me to where I am today. I sometimes think I'm dreaming and it's the most beautiful dream, but I'm not! I fought long and hard to get out from under the devil's lair, and without the help of many people who could have simply turned their backs on me, I wouldn't have made it. Now I'm only left with the question of why? but Isn't this the question we are all left with after all of this? WHY are over 100,000 people (most of whom are under the age of 30) dying every year in our country when they simply don't have to? WHY, when we are living in the 21st century, is there anything that we are allowing to kill our citizens, our CHILDREN, OUR FUTURE!! I'm so sick and tired of watching all these movies and documentaries about opioid addiction and seeing the tremendous pain and devastation on the faces of parents who have lost their children or other loved ones to this devastating disease, Yes I said DISEASE because that's exactly what it is a DISEASE!! In the 1950s the medical field included ADDICTION as a disease! Let me repeat this one more time because it's the most important part of this entire book. This addiction is a DISEASE, IT'S NOT A MORAL ISSUE OR SOMETHING SOMEONE CHOOSES!! IT CHOOSES YOU! A disease, just like cancer, hypertension, heart disease, crohn's disease, Huntington disease, Parkinsons, Alzheimers, ALS, muscular dystrophy and the 1000s of others! I didn't choose this disease, it CHOSE ME. Dr. William Leach, which I hope, if this book gets any notoriety at all, Becomes the face and the voice, and the utmost educated expert on addiction in America that HE IS and shows everyone a proven track record and solid way to defeat it! I hope people use his savior-like ability to handle this addiction disease to their advantage! It's very simple this man SAVED MY LIFE, not only by treating my addiction, but more importantly educating me beforehand about how he would do it and what it would involve from me, which honestly was mostly just time. No long withdrawals or cravings ever again! Just time and a strong desire to live a normal life again!. He simply told me if I followed his directions, and followed his steps exactly as he told me, my life could be saved and I could live a completely normal productive life again!. I did, and it was! Again, I wasn't special and he can do the same thing for you and/or your loved ones, he can save their lives as well! He can and will give you and your loved ones a proven blueprint on how to give their lives back to them and your families!! He understands it's a disease, not a moral issue! He didn't simply see me as another drug addict thats life was worthless anyway, so why save it? He saw me as a person, a human being that had a dreaded disease that he could help rid me of! He told me out of 100 people who get prescribed opioids for the first time, 88 can take the medication as directed and never want and/ or crave it ever again in their lives. The 12% left are like me and are born with an addictive gene that makes my entire genealogy susceptible to this disease called addiction! I and millions of others simply have a disease. A disease, that, unless we get our heads out of our asses and start proactively doing something about, is going to kill millions more and go down as the deadliest disease ever known to humanity! If you had cancer, or say, multiple sclerosis and I told you that you could take one pill a day and stave it off for the rest of your life and you could live a completely normal life, would you take it? Do I need to even ask such a preposterous question? That's exactly what I do every day. I take one pill to control my addiction disease! I have taken Suboxone every day for over 10 years and my life gets better daily, and I have had no type of withdrawals, nor once craved an opioid drug, EVER!! Am I any different from the guy that has hypertension and takes a blood pressure pill every day? Let me answer that for you, NO IM NOT!! Am I any different from the lady that takes a cholesterol pill daily to control her cholesterol DISEASE! Again, NO! Or the diabetic that takes insulin daily. Again, no I'm not! I have a disease in which I take a daily pill to control, again People might say, well, he's traded one drug for another and my answer to that is you're just ignorant to what you're talking about and poorly educated about the subject you're speaking on! My life, as you have just read, was in complete shambles before Suboxone. I DON'T GET HIGH AND I DON'T WANT TO GET HIGH! I was at a crossroads in time in my life, life or death, and I chose life, to try my hardest not to do pain pills anymore, and try Suboxone, and it LITERALLY saved my life! I'M LIVING PROOF GUYS, COME ON! TEN YEARS COMPLETELY CLEAN!! A complete 10+ year study PROVING Suboxone can save millions of lives, just as it has mine!!! Lets save MILLIONS of lives and get this disease under what control we can. There are only appx 40,000 doctors that can prescribe Suboxone in the United States and over a million doctors that can prescribe opioids. You guys do the math and if you can't, let me break it down as simply as I can! We as a society are literally killing millions and millions of people by not making this medication available to anyone and everyone willing to try it to cure and maintain their disease, and keep it under control so they too can live normal productive lives! Same thing a diabetic does each day with insulin: take a pill that maintains their disease. What's really insane is we are supplying FREE naloxone to people for WHEN they overdose, so why not give them something that will prevent the damn overdose in the first place and give their lives back to them, as well as their loved ones!!! We are murdering our citizens, our children, and our future as a country! I will get on the highest mountain top and preach, scream, and raise more hell than anyone. you know if I'm ever given any type of platform to reach people, trust me. As Doc Holliday famously once said, "I'll be your huckleberry". And I give you all my word, I will! My dream would be to go in front of congress and tell them my story and also inform them that if we as a country can make this cure for addiction obtainable and affordable, we as a society can save millions of lives! It really is that simple! If this book falls into the hands of anyone who can make this happen, let's do it! As you have read, I have a very compelling TRUE story about how Suboxone, along with a very educated Addiction specialist, Dr William Leach, again literally saved my life! I know of course there will be mountains to climb and valleys to go through, but WE can save millions of lives! Think about that for a minute. MILLIONS OF LIVES! However many years I have left on this earth, I will dedicate myself to saving as many lives as I can with my message! I will be our HUCKLEBERRY! I also want to leave you with the hope and inspiration that you will beat this thing and you will get back to your normal life you had before opiates. It's difficult! It's by far the most difficult thing you will ever do in your life! You're going to have to dig the deepest you ever have inside yourself, your body, mind and soul to escape, but YOU CAN, Simply because I did, and I was, and I am exactly who you are. Another person trapped in a dreaded disease! I just hope one day I can be OUR huckleberry! I have made a bunch of song references in my book, but I have saved the most important until now, the end of my story. When I was teetering on the razor's edge, I would always listen to my favorite song of all time. Peace train by cat stevens. Whatever you're doing right now, google the lyrics and listen to the song, it's amazing! The lyrics say it all and always pumped hope and inspiration into me just when I needed it most!

"Get your bags together, come bring your good friends too. "

Our cause is getting nearer, it soon will be with you,

And come join the living, it's not too far from you,

And it's getting nearer, soon it will all be true,

Cause out on the edge of darkness, there rides a Peace Train,

Oh, peace train, take my soul, come take me home again."

" JP out ", and May god be with us all and may god bless America!

THE END

Made in United States
Troutdale, OR
11/30/2024